Shehy Mts
1798
Glengariff
Owvane R.
Ballyneen
Dunmanway
Bandon
Bantry
Whiddy I.
Mts. of
Durrus
Timol
Clonakilty
Blairs Cove
Mt. Gabriel
R. Ilen
Ross Carbery
Skibbereen
Gubbeen Dairy
Glandore
Glandore Harbor
Unionhall
Rosscarbery
Rosscarbery Bay
Galley
Castletownsend
Castle Haven
Toe Head
Stags
Baltimore
Kedge I.
Sherkin I.
Clear I.
Cape Clear
alf Isles
QUEENSTOWN TO NEW YORK 2,728 MILES
300
LANTIC

GUBBEEN

Gubbeen is a 250-acre, traditional farm on the most south-westerly tip of Ireland and is renowned for its award-winning cheese (called Gubbeen) and its smoked meats. This book encompases the four voices of the farm – Giana, Tom, Fingal and Clovisse – and what they do, from looking after their animals (poultry, pigs and cows), to cheesemaking, smoking meats and growing biodynamic vegetables.

Giana manages the dairy as well as keeping a keen eye on the poultry; Tom has worked the land all his life, following the old farming traditions of his forbearers; their son Fingal creates his own salamis, chorizo, hams and bacon in the Smokehouse while their daughter Clovisse, a cook, tends to the Kitchen Garden, feeding the family, guests and local restaurants with her salads, herbs and vegetables.

Nothing is wasted and the circle of life sustains the family whilst creating the highest quality products for speciality shops around the world. In this insightful book they share their stories, practical advice and delicious recipes for you to enjoy.

GUBBEEN

THE STORY OF A WORKING FARM

WITH RECIPES FROM THE DAIRY, SMOKEHOUSE AND KITCHEN GARDEN

GIANA FERGUSON

& CLOVISSE FERGUSON

PHOTOGRAPHY BY ANDY SEWELL

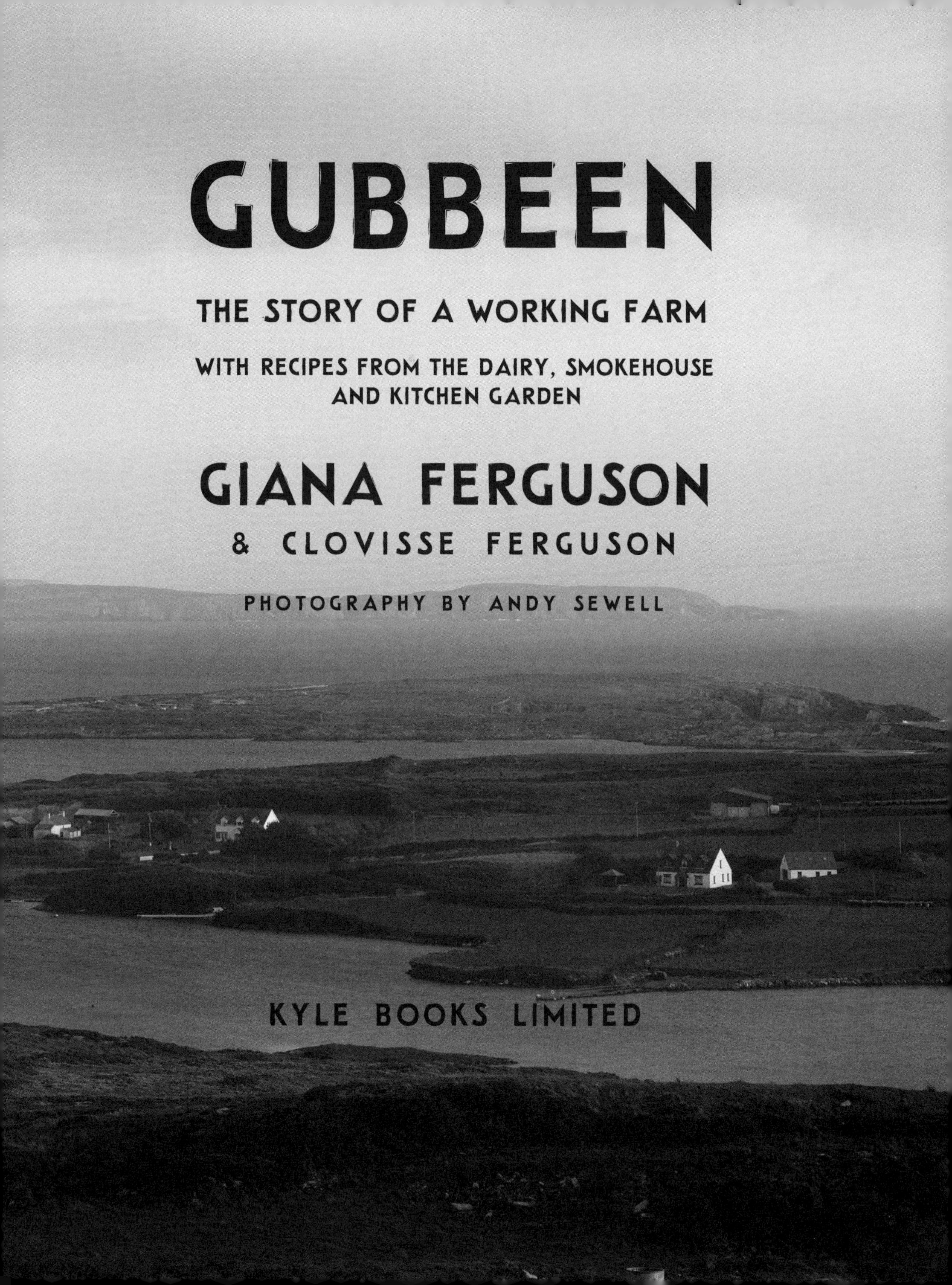

KYLE BOOKS LIMITED

CONTENTS

TO MYRTLE ALLEN, CHRIS JEPSON

& VERONICA STEELE

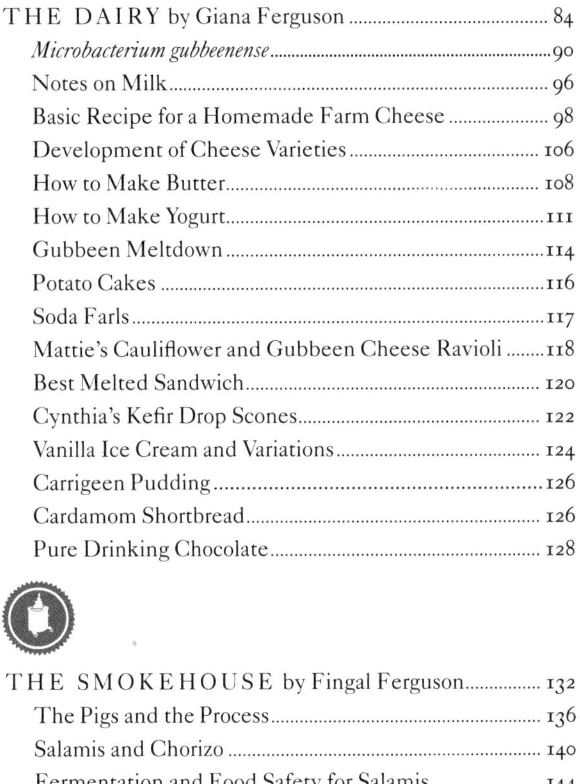

FOREWORD

Gubbeen kitchen is one of those rare and special places where one just feels warm, content and at peace with the world. If I close my eyes I'm sitting at the timber table with my back to the wall. Long, lanky, handsome Tom comes in from milking his herd of Friesian and Kerry cows, clutching a jug of fresh creamy milk for breakfast. He lifts up the cover of the ancient Aga and slides across the huge aluminium kettle; soon there will be rashers and eggs with thick slices of toast and a fine pot of Barry's tea. Little Olan and Oscar dart around, Giana brings in a bowl of eggs fresh from the hens; maybe there will be a duck egg – Tom's favourite. Clovisse, who has created a little Garden of Eden down beside her brother Fingal's smokehouse, is assembling a cheese wedding cake for an order. Rosie arrives and then Fingal's wife Ciara walks around the corner with Euan, the youngest grandchild, in her arms. The dressers in this beautiful country kitchen are laden with an eclelctic mix of family treasures and Giana's 'finds'.

Here is a Irish farming family, three generations that love and nurture the land that has been passed down from father to son and, eventually, to grandson and great grandson. They have found their own way to survive and prosper, so they can live on the beautiful West Cork land that they love. In 1975, Giana decided to try her hand at cheesemaking, with some of the surplus milk, at a time when we were all a nation of 'Calvita eaters' – the beautiful, wrinkly, washed rind cheese became known as Gubbeen after the townland where it was made. The Fergusons were early pioneers, adding value to the produce on the farm with a clear vision to produce fresh seasonal food for their customers and devotees.

Fingal, in his early 20s, followed his parents' lead and began to experiment with curing and charcuterie. He built a smokehouse and became an inspiration for many young artisan producers. Like his parents, Fingal continues to innovate with a deep respect for tradition, and now produces over 50 products, much of which he sells directly to customers at the local farmers' markets of Schull, Bantry, Mahon and Skibbereen.

His sister Clovisse has inherited green fingers and is now a biodynamic gardener with a terraced acre and several tunnels below the Gubbeen farmhouse, which grow a wide variety of beautiful salads, vegetables and fresh herbs, supply local chefs and flavour the cures for Fingal's smoked meats. Her delicious Summer Garden Lunches in the Gubbeen kitchen enable guests to enjoy a taste of everything that the farm produces.

Giana also has a deep love and fascination for poultry, hatching rare breeds in her collection of incubators on Tom's grandmother's fine mahogany table in the dining room – chicken and ducks of every hue, Bronze Turkeys and Toulouse Cross Geese in spring – and then reunites them with their parents who rear them naturally in the orchard behind Gubbeen House.

This West Cork family of artisan producers are a symbol of what can be achieved when a family works together to add value to the beautiful produce on their farm. In just a few decades the name Gubbeen has become synonymous with superb quality artisan produce, both here in Ireland and abroad, and I'm so delighted that their inspirational story has been written, so it can continue to intrigue others.

Darina Allen, Ballymaloe Cookery School

Birthday

1

THE LAND

GUBBEEN lies between Mount Gabriel and the Atlantic Ocean on County Cork's Mizen Peninsula, the most south-westerly point of Ireland.

This farm and its townland – or geographical division of land named in Gaelic long before the Norman invasion – is from *Gob*, meaning mouth; and the Goibin, little mouthful, is the inlet down at Crewe Bay below us from where for generations the Fergusons would have brought seaweed up to fertilise the land, just as my daughter Clovisse does today.

In spring and summer much of the mountain is covered in highly flammable furze (gorse), stingingly yellow and smelling of coconut biscuits. Late spring brings out the shepherds who burn off the furze and the ling (heather), which has become a tight, dry underbrush and goes up like firelighters. The evenings see tongues of fire running along the mountain, filling the air with the smell of turf and coconut.

The Ice Age tore down to the Atlantic, leaving our land covered in exposed rock ridges and pockets of wet, but fertile, acidic bog. We sometimes muse about going to the islands just offshore from Gubbeen and asking for our topsoil back – this is where the ice melted and deposited its riches. There the land is so fertile they can grow 2 tons of grain to the acre, whereas we are pressed to grow 1.5 tons. Even after years of applying manure and seaweed our topsoil is shallow and the clay underneath holds water.

The names of these islands will be no strangers to you – Long Island, Coney Island and, looking back to the east, there is Baltimore. The significance of these names isn't lost hereabouts: the steady exodus of the people going west to find work, and the hope of wealth to send home, took with them the memory of their land and transplanted it as soon as they could onto their new landscape. They left gaping holes in families along this shoreline. It also left the sense of our neighbouring parish being America.

We have ancient potato ridges from the famine times on one small part of the high ground and they are left untouched, the soil never reddened or ploughed out of respect for the land and the people of that time.

In our bog there are several Fualact Fia, old Iron Age gathering places and eating grounds where stones were collected into pits and fires set on top, there foods were boiled for the Fir Bolg people who lived in this tough place. These were strong, little, hairy people, my husband Tom says, and clearly hunter gatherers. There would have been wolves back then and, I believe, bears – these places we protect too. Before so many people left, these bogs provided turf for fires and this land was grazed by sheep or beef cattle. Now with modern drainage, the fertility of the bog has improved and we graze our heifers there.

So this is our northern boundary, the bog with this significant mountain, Mount Gabriel, as the backdrop. On its peak is a very modern and rather beautiful piece of 21st-century engineering: two geodesic domes that house aircraft radar. They

are the design of the late futurist and humanist, Buckminster Fuller, and his understanding of continuous tension being a foil to Atlantic winds. To us, they are also beautiful, and somehow a beacon to more than the equipment they protect; they seem to be relevant to the people of West Cork who have long embraced other cultures and enjoy original thinkers.

Our land runs back to the foothills of Mount Gabriel and bounds the straight road to Crookhaven. These fields, all drained now, are good pasture for the herd in the summer but are known as 'cold Corthna' as the winds whip through in the winter.

Then south, below our farm, is the Atlantic, where on the sunny summer days the sea is full of yachts coming from regattas along this ideal sailing coast, all working the currents and wind off the famous Carbery's Hundred Isles. If you drew a line from the top of Mount Gabriel through our land due west, you would hit, 10 nautical miles out to sea, the Fastnet Lighthouse, another

beacon, this one a sign throughout the years that seafarers had made it across the Atlantic from America. The lighthouse, no longer manned, is still very dramatic and the seas out there are not for any but the most experienced – on stormy nights the breakers rise up to its top light. Every 5 seconds the beam cuts through and lights our windows, a pulse in the place that would bring a real sense of loss were it ever to stop.

This most south-westerly tip of Ireland is the Mizen Peninsula, the parish of Schull and our townland of Gubbeen. It is an extreme place to be farming, perhaps, but it has always supported families, our own for six generations now. It has always attracted visitors and travellers: the Vikings, Spanish, Huguenots, English and, finally in the 70s, hippies, as they were called then. A migration of young, well-educated people escaping the Cold War in Europe, and Maggie Thatcher's policies in the UK. One population census of that time showed a spike that referenced a fair number of families who were living with outdoor plumbing, but who had several members with degrees, some even with doctorates. These people have become devoted members of the West Cork community, bringing their creativity with music festivals, Buddhist centres, art galleries, bookshops and, of course, organic foods and farming principles to this peninsula. We call it the Levant of Ireland.

Perhaps it is not surprising that such a coast attracted pirates, fishermen, tourists and traders. What is so special is that the local people were so open-minded, welcoming and civilised that they could absorb it all and develop as a community of intelligent, creative, honorable people who above all educated their children and worked the land and seas to benefit one another. Similarly, the philosophers, poets and priests who turned up here throughout our history were mostly honoured and supported, and in return they added their cultural dimension. This, I feel, is why we are thriving today, the bars still fuel brilliant conversation and visitors are met with courtesy and a curiosity about their life and who they are.

As so many newcomers here are escapists, from success as well as failure, there is at times a need for a level of local tolerance. When a visiting magistrate sat in Schull Court in the late 70s, he awarded a small fine and some advice to a young man sporting a badge on his lapel with the words, 'Don't panic, it's organic'. He'd been living on an island and was arrested for possessing a shopping bag full of homegrown dope. The magistrate wanted to know why the offender was not satisfied with the traditional vices of our country, whiskey and stout. How reasonable.

So, for us, Gubbeen embodies this land and its history. The farm is 250 adjusted acres, with an old double-roofed Georgian squireen's house surrounded by trees that shelter us from the wind and give us privacy. It is where we work the land and it is where we daily, all of us, make food. We farm traditionally – Tom has always managed this land with his belief in being a steward only for his lifetime; he doesn't see it as a possession, or as a means to profit. He says that it seems to him a good idea to remember what your grandfather and father got right, so you can support your children and grandchildren to inherit the place in better shape than when it came to you. He and his father William followed this belief and they are the reason why the foods now made at Gubbeen came about. Not only did they encourage some of the early dreams, but they worked alongside us with the first efforts, and brought to the development their skills as farmers who have to be architects, plumbers and logistical engineers every day, and that is before they even start to be carpenters, mechanics and parents.

The first member of the Ferguson family in Schull arrived on a bicycle all the way from Carrickfergus in County Antrim where he could have traced their line back to the early Ulster Plantations from Scotland. He came to Lowertown – named after the luachair or golden rush-like grass that grows on top of bogs in the autumn. He brought with him some tea to sell and an agency for a machine known as a milk separator. This allowed him to set up a small creamery, important because this separating of milk into skim (for feeding their calves) and cream, gave local farmers the opportunity to join

the Butter Markets. In the 1880s, Ireland was Britain's number one supplier of butter, almost a third of which was produced in Cork. Much of it was packed in small wooden boxes, sent by tram along the straight 'butter roads' of West Cork and Kerry and travelled via the Butter Exchange in Cork, on by ship to Liverpool and then to the West Indies, Brazil and Australia. Schull had a station for the butter carriage to Cork. Tom's childhood memory is that this tram travelled slightly faster than a donkey, but not as fast as a bicycle.

So, in 1975, just after our marriage, with this heritage of cream and butter and blessed with a little mouthful of land, Tom's skills as a dairy farmer and my love of food and farming, we embarked on the adventure of cheesemaking. Our formula is simple: the grass grows to feed the herd, their milk comes into the dairy where we make cheese, and the by-product, the whey, is fed to the pigs that provide the meat for our son Fingal's charcuterie. Clovisse, our daughter, has been the gardener and herb grower, destiny perhaps after spending her childhood trotting behind her grandfather in his vegetable garden at Gubbeen, with a certain new twist in her garden plan reinforced by training in organic horticulture and the influence of some great gardeners, but still driven by a love of food. She is now a cook and developer of food products from our farm for both the family table and tourism.

Along with neighbours and friends we have all developed the local farmers' markets that grew out of the old traditional fairs and the wonderful country markets that have always flourished in this area. Our 'new' foods are in part the result of the many cultures here, but they come especially from the strong generations of attachment of the farmers and fishermen who worked the land and sea for so long before us.

Back when the kids were skipping to the old chant, 'Yum, yum, pig's bum, cabbage and potataaas!', there was a timely warning that 'Aristocrats, like pigs' heads, will be frowned upon, and noodle soup will threaten Irish stew.' This has been heeded at Gubbeen, where pig's bum and cabbage are honoured: one of our family favourites is ham with Clovisse's brassica salad, and Fingal will return from the abattoir with his pigs' heads to transform them with hours of work for his brawn. Fingal and Clovisse are both very much a product of our West Cork farm, but with something of a Buckminster Fuller spirit behind them.

How this family works and how Gubbeen manages to produce foods that are now finding their way all over the world is a fun, if rather exhausting, story. It starts in the land the Fergusons have worked for several hundred years and is the excuse for these pages, these recipes and these ideas that Tom, Fingal, Clovisse and I have developed.

Tom Ferguson

Farming Gubbeen

Getting up early is something people associate with farming. Do they see it as a sacrifice maybe? For me, it has never seemed that way; it is what my family has always done, and we see it as a privilege.

There is so much life before dawn that you can feel around you as you go out, so many creatures that share our farm with us. When you step out into the morning darkness and head to the cow shed, the heat and the scent of cattle waiting for their morning milking is a quiet, peaceful and private time. Cows are reasonable, gentle animals and walking among them in the morning is something every dairy farmer will view as time well spent in good company. I would know each animal in the herd from the moment they were born, on through their weaning and feeding in the sheds and then, when they calve themselves and become part of the milking herd we are still meeting each morning and evening. Rearing animals is a daily routine, day in, day out, but one that gives the rhythm to our way of life.

In spring and summer months, before dawn, when I am bringing in the herd to milk from the pasture, the odd lights will be on in the hills around, young mothers woken by their babies perhaps, or other milkers starting their day. From every field at Gubbeen there is a different view. I often see my daughter-in-law Ciara out walking with the children on her side of the hill, taking them to school. Beyond the farm and out to sea, the Fastnet Lighthouse is always awake, if not so alive now that it is automated as it was when Geoff McCarthy was lighthouse keeper, but it is a permanent marker nonetheless. On a clear morning you will see fishing trawlers heading off to the fishing grounds, and along the horizon the odd oil tanker plying its trade too.

First thing in the morning I often meet the wild creatures that live among our animals. They are the nocturnal residents scurrying about the farmyard: badgers, bats, foxes, mice, pigeons, mink, feral cats and rats. The most successful species change depending on their relationship with each other and our farming methods. Wherever there is man, on farms or in cities, there will always be rats. In the mornings I hear them in the barn or up in the feed bins, working to outwit Giana with new ways of breaking into her chickenfeed, or making off with the calf nuts.

The fox too is always around and of a morning as I come into the yard there is always that dread that I will find a trail of feathers of some foolish old hen that didn't go in with her flock and has paid the ultimate price. Magpies are the natural competitor to the fox, both opportunistic predators battling it out for the pickings in the yards. The magpies – such dreadful sneaks – have learnt to tell tales on the foxes by following them along the hedgerows, signalling to me with their hacking call. I imagine this is to alert me that the fox is there; how the guileful, stealthy fox must hate them!

Deprived of the chance to lure a duck to stick its poor old head out of the wire of its safe cage, they have to slink away to hunt in the wild once I am up. Foxes are no longer so frightened of humans as they used to be: they have learnt to raid dustbins, and some summer visitors will leave food out for them. So with all this extra food about foxes have proliferated. I am seeing more of them during hard winters with diseases, which I suspect comes from closer contact with people. A British veterinary journal published a review on urban foxes that scavenge in dustbins. They suffer from obesity, echoing problems associated with the modern human diet: too much fat, too much sugar, and too much food in general.

Gubbeen is also home to a large colony of little bats that have lived here much longer than I have; I remember them always living safely in the house roof. They are completely silent in flight, but as the first light starts to rise out west beyond the house, you sense this flickering traffic jam as they jostle to get back into the dark of our roof and hide away from the sun and noise of the farming day.

We decided to support them by never using wood preservative in our roof beams in case it poisoned the roosting colony, so when we noticed bees outside our bedroom window apparently flying in and out under the joists, the image of a couple of kilos of furious bees landing on our bed, and the possibility of literally coming to a sticky end, sent us in search of a ladder and our friend Connie O'Mahony who broke through the plaster ceiling. His torch showed the little bats hanging there, plus a tidy beehive, but, above all, it showed the structure of the roof: fine, impressive beams, pinned at the apex with wooden pegs. Clearly visible on these beams were long, grooved tracks which could only be one thing – barnacle scars. I find great comfort in this strength of the original house. When south-westerly gales batter Gubbeen during winter, it is nice to know that our roof was designed and built by men who understood how to build boats. Knowing that our ancestors would have had wreck rights, and that our beams came from a time when old sailing ships that foundered off Fastnet were salvaged and the deck cargo brought here to build our home, gives us a sense of permanence.

My great-grandfather William bought Gubbeen as it is today for my grandfather Thomas Ferguson when he married. They had four sons, of whom my father William was the eldest. Then, the family worked a mill, and also owned a threshing machine. At harvest time the machine was dragged on a sleigh by the horses from farm to neighbouring farm. A steam engine turned the great belt that drove the thresher and separated the straw from the chaff and grain, providing sacks of oats and barley to get the animals through the winter. When I think of the changes in health and safety standards in my lifetime, this work was high risk. During a day's threshing, the spinning drum on top of the machine was big enough to chop a grown man in half in seconds; there was drinking, there were belts flying and kids running in and out under this huge machine, but, miracle or not, no one was hurt.

Not long after the Second World War, my father William had a tractor sent down from County Meath and, for a while, Gubbeen was the first farm on the peninsula to have this engine power. There was still the blockade at sea and no rubber was imported into Ireland for tyres. I remember the big grooved iron wheels. Until recently those wheels were leaning up against a wall in the haggard (farmyard), in perfect condition, a monument to the good engineering and materials of those days. For my father, the transition to machines was painless; he was a natural mechanic and admired the progress offered by machines. And, thankfully, it was the beginning of the end of some of the back-breaking work.

While the investment in that first tractor supported the continuation of self-sufficiency for the local townland, it also marked the start of our petro-chemical dependency.

In my father's time, Gubbeen had worked eight horses, all stabled in the lower yard. The horses were used here until the mid-1950s, working alongside the tractor. The last mare, a grey, was kept on for potato drilling, tackled up and walked into the field to open the well-cultivated, manured soil into ridges. On the morning of planting we would cut each well-chitted seed potato into three seeds, which were placed into the drill ploughed 9 inches deep. The mare would retrace her steps between the two planted rows and 'split' the original drill, covering both lines of the planted seeds. To allow the potato shoots to come through, a large, rough blackthorn bush was tied onto the mare's tackle so she could drag it along the ridge tops to brush off excess earth.

I went to a local primary school and then to Midleton College, a boarding school in East Cork. During the holidays, as soon as I could work, I was doing stuff around the farm; nobody gave a thought back then if they saw a nine-year-old driving on the main road to the creamery. They would say then, 'Put the young and the weak ones in the tractor, let them drive; any fella that can work stays on the ground!'

Growing up on a farm, you see and learn how to do everything instinctively. When I think of my grandfather and his time as custodian of Gubbeen I remember how he managed the land and the skills that still influence what we do here every day. It makes me a very happy man to see my grandchildren now starting to watch and observe the farm from the seat of my tractor. And it is a real joy to have watched our two children, Fingal and Clovisse, continue to develop their own interests in farming, while Rosie Gingell spent many years driving about in machines fifty times her size with such skill, fearlessly leading bulls across fields and spending endless nights feeding the heifers and then their calves.

My mother, Mary Ferguson, died when I was eighteen. She was an amazing lady, a founding member of the ICA (Irish Countrywoman's Association) and as much of an innovator as my father. When I was a child she started one of the first farm guesthouses in Ireland, around the same time that Myrtle and Ivan Allen started Ballymaloe House in East Cork.

In the summertime, my sisters and I were all kicked into the back rooms and the whole house would be packed full of guests. When I came home from school for the summer, I would take over the farm as my father became chief bottle washer for the guesthouse. On occasions there might have been twelve to fourteen guests staying at Gubbeen; they would book a two-week holiday, sharing a communal living room. Dinner was served in the dining room every evening, cooked by my mother, and my father would carve the meat. It was a bit like Johnny Desmond's Island Cottage Restaurant out on Heir Island now: if it was chicken on the menu, it was chicken they got. It was a risky business, never knowing whether all the guests would get along, but it seemed to work very well.

Gubbeen is recognised as being a relatively self-sufficient farm, but until the 1960s farming in West Cork was naturally self-sufficient.

There was a sort of creed, simply that you never wasted anything. Even today I can find pieces of machines in the back of our shed that my father put aside 'just in case'. Nothing was bought in, there was no fertiliser, no feed. Farmers had to grow their own turnips and beets and grains; there were no central creamery shops then. We would always convert any surplus into supplies for hungrier times. Until the deep freezer came along, my mother made every jam, chutney and preserve I can think of, including preserved eggs. She used to store them in a big battery jar and use them for baking; they became a little runny perhaps, but they were there for her in winter when there was nothing else.

There are only about ten people in our area, from here to Skibbereen, who have pigs now. We always kept them at Gubbeen, and they were a key part of the diversity of the farming systems of this area. Everybody had a pig then: on a Tuesday all the farmers would be at the mart in Skibbereen where 300 to 400 bonhams (piglets) per week would change hands. It takes a lot of work and skill to make any money from a pig today, but there was always a few extra bob in a litter while I was growing up. I remember our neighbour Pat Wholley saying that 'cows put the food on the table, but the pigs educated the children'.

Much like the systems that Clovisse has started in her garden, seeds were always saved and never wasted. The chosen barley seed for next year's planting would be taken from the field with the highest yield, sacked up and protected in the loft until the following spring. I would see old neighbours, Johnny and Paddy O'Driscoll, walking the land every evening, checking fences and water troughs. In his pocket, Johnny would have a handful of sweepings from his hay shed and, as he walked, he would scatter these back on his land to fill patches of empty ground, reseeding his hay meadow for the following year.

At home in Gubbeen, the barley grain was brought in from the harvest and stored loose on the floor of the loft beside the house. My grandmother would store her vegetable marrows in this pile of grain too, a good dry place to preserve them through long winters. I remember one of her generous, delicious dishes for big harvest suppers was one of these huge marrows cut in half and stuffed with either minced beef or lamb that had been cooked with onions, sage and thyme, then covered in breadcrumbs and baked in the oven.

During winter, milling was one of the many jobs that sustained the family. Many of our neighbours would bring their sacks of grain, by horse and cart, for milling. Below the loft was our mill and the grain would be drawn up to the loft and dropped down into the hod to be ground. The hammer mill could screen to various shapes and sizes, depending on what we were using the grain for: oats for the animals, or wheat for baking, fine flour for cakes or coarser flour for bread.

As winter drew to a close, and the pile of grain receded, room was made for us to start laying out the seed potatoes for chitting, waiting for the little sprouts to appear as the weather warmed up. We had about five varieties of potatoes that we would grow, starting with 'Home Guard' followed by 'Sharp's Express'. Although vulnerable to blight, the delicious, floury 'Kerr's Pink' were our more preferred crop, while later came 'Iron Victors' and 'King Edward'. Our first experience of imported seeds was when Joe Newman, a merchant naval officer my father knew, brought back purple potatoes from South America.

These potato crops were not always without problems. Some, of course, would fail with the blight, though others we could store right through the winter in pits dug in the field, then lined with straw. These were then covered up with sods of earth to keep them airtight. Again the main enemy was rats robbing the pits.

There was no artificial fertiliser, apart from 'slag' – a combination of lime and phosphate rock. As Gubbeen is a coastal farm, every year seaweed was laid down, all by hand from batches hauled up from the strand by horse and cart. Farmyard manures from cattle, poultry and pigs were a truly valuable asset. These would be stored as composting heaps in the yards, then carted off to the land in the spring.

A key transitional time for a farm like Gubbeen was when Ireland joined the EU,

and agricultural incomes trebled overnight. Nitrogen was introduced to release the 'hidden acres' promised by the national farm advisers, who encouraged its use as a key to building Irish agriculture. Huge grants suddenly became available for reclamation of land and every farmer went legs first for it. Including Gubbeen.

As young dairy farmers in the 1970s we made our income via a contract with Baileys Irish Cream, a landmark business whose markets grew so fast that they were shipping milk from here in West Cork all the way up to Virginia, County Cavan. By the early 1980s, European subsidies had created a wine lake, a milk lake and a well-stocked Irish butter mountain.

It spelt the end of self-sufficiency, and we abandoned all of our old practices and went straight to dairying. A milking parlour was built and within five years we went from 25 milking cows to 100. As we increased our number of cattle, we dropped grain production, because by then very good concentrates from the Co-Op had become available. Winter cattle feeding became easier and we substituted our feed with big clamps of self-feeding silage in our yards. By now the entire farm was turned over to grass production for our milking herd.

As a young couple, with our children just going to school, Giana and I had some sense of financial security at last. At the same time,

we both instinctively knew that we wanted an independence and freedom from the global markets that were opening up. This was when Giana's culture came into play: we should farm for food, not commodities; were we prepared to take that risk and to work as food makers? I can still hear her saying, 'With all our milk, why can't we make food? We should make cheese: traditional, hand-made cheese from our land.' For her, with the experience of a childhood spent in France and Spain, it was obvious; for me it was for a while a risk, but one worth taking.

Giana's love of the European food that she had grown up with, and driven by the sense that in Ireland we deserved the same richness of local food culture we knew from time spent in France and Spain, this was something we both so wanted to develop in our own home. We knew we wanted an alternative to bulk tanks and grants. We believed that, with our combined skills and energy, we could do this and, just as crucial, we could produce a complex and interesting cheese for the Irish market. It was 1978. It has been a struggle at times, it has always been an adventure, but, most important, now it seems to be a reality for the future for our farm.

Farmers' Markets

Change is part of farming – nothing stays the same and, even though the work of each day is to try to maintain some consistency for the animals and ourselves, we always need to keep thinking about the future.

Some years ago, we moved out of selling directly to supermarkets and into developing farmers' markets. I can't remember whether it was Giana or I who first felt that being drawn into central marketing would be a disadvantage for us, being such a small-production food business. On the one hand we knew we might isolate ourselves, but as we had developed a strong customer list by the time the children were leaving school, we knew this was the time to risk a move to market Gubbeen products independently.

It took a bit of courage to force ourselves off the farm at first and to confront the market directly, but as a relatively small supplier, it made complete sense to sell direct to our customers.

I had been familiar with fairs and local markets from a young age; I grew up selling cattle and pigs at these marts. There was no food sold then, only animals. That our farm now produces foods that sell locally makes sense to me and to our visitors and neighbours. I knew the importance of long-term relationships and the trust that would be needed to develop over time with our neighbours, other producers and new customers, if we were to succeed with these markets.

There is so much more going on at markets than selling food, just as, when I was young, going to the creamery was more than delivering milk. There is no denying that farming is usually a solitary business; perhaps we prefer to work alone, making our mistakes in private. Heading off into town with our produce was a big step. Setting up our stall at a market brings the great advantage of picking up on the world outside our fences. Sharing our work with neighbours and talking about the way we farm have become a major part of my week. That I have a lot of experience with logistics, and knowing about machinery, helps greatly: I am never daunted by managing the stocks or having to nurse a van into life on a cold morning or a broken fridge back to work on the hot summer days.

When we started the farmers' markets and our foods were being bought for the first time, we got direct feedback from customers, especially children. Fingal called them his 'R&D Department', and they were often spot-on with their criticism! He would line them up like birds on the crossbar of our trestle table and have them taste new pepperoni recipes he had learnt in Italy or Spain. I am particularly pleased that so many children come to our stall; they have amazing palates and are very open-minded about trying new foods.

There are now four main markets a week where we sell locally. On any given day I might be buying pigs one minute or struggling with the stall umbrella in gale-force winds the next. No matter what the weather there are always customers lined up with shopping

bags and wanting some of our cheese, or Fingal's meats, or Clovisse's tarts or salads. It is hugely satisfying. Our customers have built these markets alongside us, they are very important to us and the ties are very close.

Now that farmers' markets have been established in our local towns, it seems to me that these are the places where many of the changes to our West Cork culture are debated and forged, which explains why they are such a key part of our life and now our communities.

The Kitchen

A farm kitchen is the focus of the house. It is the first port of call for everyone, and at times ours seems to have more traffic than most as it has three doors. There is always someone coming in from the farm with mucky boots doing that tip-toe thing that people do when they don't want to take off dirty boots. The floor has big black and white tiles so walking on the black tiles is the dance we all do, leaving tracks across the black tiles as we make our way to the office off the kitchen, the source of all the paperwork, cheque books and references we always seem to need endlessly during the day's work.

There are always toddlers too, trying to make a break for the sitting room and the lure of cartoons. Heading them off before they make it out of the kitchen is their game – it has become a sort of race and if they make it to the hall and the sanctuary of the door to the sitting room they feel they have moral grounds for some telly time.

This is always a warm room, the Aga gently humming away, usually with a kettle simmering on it. This Aga is now well into its third generation and a magnet for anyone who is cold or wants to talk, they hitch themselves onto the rail and hold court from there. In the evenings the dogs line up along the Aga; during the day they also try for the cushions on the two table end chairs, and it is a game of chicken to see who will sit on a dog, or whether they can slip out from under a descending human just in time.

This kitchen has always fed the family and often the people who work with us, too. The people who come to help at harvest time and in the dairy as it grew would all come in for lunch, so many at one point that we invested in two dishwashers.

So, a three-ringed circus all day, a room with a constant flow of food, talk and cooking, with really rather a lot of traffic in and out, and at night when the sun goes down and the cooking starts with a glass of wine, the chopping and peeling done on the table, then the kitchen becomes something quite else, a really private and quiet place where you can hear the clock ticking.

Pizza

When Fingal built his bread oven, we all shared his dream, some of us for breads, some of us for meat cooked in great heat with a wonderful pink centre, but all of us were looking forward to great pizzas. Here's how we make them.

MAKES 6–8 MEDIUM PIZZAS

- 1kg white bread flour, plus extra for dusting
- 1 teaspoon fine sea salt
- 2 × 7g sachets dried yeast
- 1 teaspoon sugar
- 4 tablespoons extra-virgin olive oil
- 550ml lukewarm water

Sift the flour and salt onto a clean work surface and make a well in the middle. Mix the yeast, sugar, olive oil and water together in a jug, leave for a few minutes to let the yeast activate, then pour into the well. Using your fingertips, gradually bring the flour in from the sides and swirl it into the liquid, bringing in larger amounts of flour until it all starts to come together. Knead until you have a smooth, nicely springy dough.

Place the ball of dough in a large, flour-dusted bowl and flour the top of it. Cover the bowl with a damp cloth and put in a warm place for 1 or 2 hours until the dough has doubled in size.

Turn out the dough onto a flour-dusted surface. Start kneading with your hands to knock back the dough (push the air out). If using straight away, divide the dough up into as many little balls as you want to make pizzas. You can also keep the dough balls, wrapped in cling film, in the fridge (or freezer) until required.

To make the pizza

Preheat the oven to 240°C/gas mark 9. Put one of your dough balls on a floured surface and start pressing and stretching from the centre of the dough, turning and pushing the dough out until you have as thin a base as possible. Place this on a floured paddle or baking tray, then add your chosen topping.

The trick to a good pizza is to keep the initial topping as basic as possible before cooking: we suggest a thin layer of passata (see page 210) and fresh buffalo mozzarella which is torn apart as opposed to sliced, or another cheese and, if you wish, perhaps a meat option, such as sliced chorizo or salami.

Cook in the oven for 5–10 minutes.

Once this is cooked you add the other ingredients, for instance: a drizzle of herb-, garlic- or chilli-infused olive oil; rocket, spinach or baby salad leaves; shaved Parmesan cheese; Parma ham; cooked mushrooms.

Our personal favourite pizza toppings

Fingal and Tom's is a tomato- and cheese-free pizza – instead using wafer-thin slices of lardo/pancetta blanco and a healthy

drizzle of herb-and-garlic-infused olive oil. Once cooked, it is top-dressed with rocket, spinach or baby salad leaves.

No surprises that I choose Quattro Formaggi as my favourite – Cashel Blue, Gubbeen, St Tola fresh goat's cheese and my most admired cheese, Comté.

Rosie's favourite is passata, fresh mozzarella, olives and marinated artichokes. Once cooked, it is topped with Serrano ham and rocket.

Clovisse's choice recalls a pizza she had in Berlin called Pizza Pazzesca – crazy pizza. It is cooked with a base topping of passata, fresh mozzarella, garlic, Italian sausage and mascarpone. Once it is out of the oven, slices of Parma ham are added.

The chef, and our friend, Lee Tiernan, chooses homemade passata, smoked Gubbeen cheese and Fingal's limited-edition rabbit salami!

A note on flour:

Make sure you use a strong white flour, one that is high in gluten, which is what you need to achieve a nice elastic dough. If you see some '00' flour pick up a bag as this is the flour Italians use to make pizza dough – it is finer-ground than normal bread flour, and it will give your dough a smooth texture. Include some semolina flour for a bit of colour and flavour if you like. You could use 1kg '00' flour, or combinations such as 800g strong white bread flour or '00' flour and 200g finely ground semolina flour.

Consommé and Bull Shots

Meaty broths are so good. My dear old grandfather, Harry Luke, in his book The Tenth Muse, *wrote pages on the origins of the great broths of the world; P.G. Woodhouse understood their significance too! We find it is not that hard to produce a seriously good consommé and of course the wicked Bull Shot (basically the same as a Bloody Mary except that it uses consommé instead of tomato juice) is impressive and a real delight. It can be drunk warm or cold – I prefer it warm.*

EQUIPMENT
Small piece of muslin
Cheesecloth

For the consommé
2 bay leaves
2 sprigs of fresh thyme
1 teaspoon cracked black pepper
2 garlic cloves, crushed
200g tomatoes, finely chopped
1 carrot, finely chopped
1 celery stick, finely chopped
1 onion, finely chopped
500g lean beef mince
5 free-range egg whites
2 litres cold beef stock
Salt

To make the consommé, tie the herbs, pepper and garlic in a piece of muslin, place with all the chopped vegetables and beef mince in a large pot over a medium heat and colour until just golden. Scrape the base of the pan periodically to prevent the ingredients from catching. Allow to cool completely, then mix in the egg whites. Add the cold beef stock, stir the mixture once, then very slowly bring up to a gentle simmer. Do not let the stock boil at any point or it will stay cloudy.

The meat and vegetables will start to float to the top to form a raft; make a small cut in the raft, when it has become firm, to let the steam out – after about 5 minutes. Gently simmer for 45 minutes to 1 hour. Season your broth with salt at this point, pinch by pinch. If you intend to reduce the consommé further after it's been strained, keep in mind that the salt will intensify as the liquid evaporates.

Place a sieve lined with cheesecloth over a second pot or a bowl. Take the consommé off the heat and gently ladle it through the cheesecloth to catch any sediment as well as the meat and vegetables. Chill the consommé as quickly as possible – you can do this by putting the broth in a heavy pot in a sink of cold water. Refrigerate until required.

For the bull shot
400ml consommé
100ml vodka
Splash of dry sherry
4 dashes of Tabasco
Generous splash of Mushroom Ketchup (see page 39) or Worcestershire sauce
Lemon juice, to taste
Celery salt
Freshly ground black pepper

For a warm Bull Shot, gently heat the consommé. Pour the vodka into 2 glasses and then the consommé. Into each glass, dash the sherry, Tabasco and mushroom ketchup and squeeze in some lemon juice to taste. Stir everything together and sprinkle with the celery salt and pepper on top.

A Bloody Bull Shot is all the above but with a 50/50 mix of consommé and passata (see page 210). This is perhaps best enjoyed cold.

Spring Lamb, Butter Beans and Dulse

Our cheesemaker and friend Rose O'Donovan and her family are shepherds and their lamb is a real spring treat. The seaweed dulse (or dilisk) is a big part of Irish tradition and has been eaten by our coastal communities for generations; together lamb and dulse are a fabulous partnership.

If you don't have any chicken stock to hand or you're just feeling extravagant (or lazy) you can use all wine. If you can't find great-quality anchovies, omit them altogether.

Note here for the wild birds: Lamb fat is not particularly good to eat in our opinion, not even to roast potatoes in, so can we suggest you give it to the birds? For each ½ cup fat add 2 tablespoons bird seed, leave it to set in a cup in your fridge, then turn it out on your bird table. The little things need a lot of fat, particularly coming up to spring when they will be nesting and laying.

SERVES **5–6**

100g butter beans
100g butter
4 medium onions, sliced
12 garlic cloves
3 healthy sprigs of thyme
Vegetable oil
1 whole shoulder of lamb, ribs removed
10 whole shallots
1 glass of white wine
Approximately 1 litre chicken stock
Salt and freshly ground black pepper

For cooking the beans
2 carrots, halved
1 celery stick
1 onion, halved
2 bay leaves
250g dulse (soaked if dried), roughly chopped
2 tablespoons olive oil
Small bunch of parsley, chopped
Juice of 1 lemon
1 tablespoon capers
1 tin good-quality anchovies (e.g. Ortez), chopped

First soak the beans overnight, covering them completely with cold water.

The next day preheat the oven to 180°C/ gas mark 4.

Place a saucepan over a low heat and add the butter, sliced onions, garlic and thyme with a pinch of salt. Cover with a lid and leave to steam.

Place a deep roasting tray over a low heat. It's handy if you have a tray large enough to accommodate the whole braise; failing that, you can transfer all the ingredients to a casserole dish before cooking in the oven.

Massage a small amount of vegetable oil all over your lamb and salt generously. Put the shoulder, skin-side down, into the tray and turn the heat up a little to encourage the lamb to fry in its rendered fat. If you do this slowly it will cook evenly, giving you a better finish. Move the shoulder around the tray so that it colours evenly, then turn it and brown the other side until the meat is golden all over.

Remove the lamb from the tray and increase the heat a notch. If the tray is swimming with fat, tip a little out.

When it is hot, add the shallots, shaking the tray. When the shallots start to colour, add the wine, stock and the steamed onions and bring to a steady bubble; check the seasoning. Nestle the shoulder back into the tray, cover with a sheet of greaseproof paper and a double layer of tinfoil, sealing the foil round the edges as best you can. Transfer to the oven and braise for 3–3½ hours.

To check your braise is ready, insert a skewer into the thickest part of the meat – it should come out as easily as it went in. It will look done now, the bones will be exposed a touch and the meat will have torn itself apart slightly. If you have time, allow the braise to rest for half hour or so; like a roasted joint it needs to relax after cooking. This also gives time for the fat to separate and rise to the top: it's good to skim a fair bit off if your lamb is particularly fatty.

About 45 minutes before the lamb comes out of the oven, drain and rinse the beans. Tip them into a large pot and cover with about 4cm water. Add the carrots, celery, halved onion and bay leaves. Bring to the boil, then turn down to a gentle simmer. Cook for about 20 minutes until tender, a little less if you like your beans with a bit of bite.

Drain the beans of their cooking liquor and discard the vegetables and bay leaves. Mix the dulce, olive oil and parsley into the beans while they are still warm. Squeeze in the lemon juice to taste, stir in the capers and anchovies and season with a touch of salt and a good grind of pepper.

Make a pillow of the beans for your lamb to lie on, or serve straight from the pans they were cooked in.

Watercress is perfect with this dish; buttered cabbage is also fantastic.

Beef Burgers

The greatest burgers are always made from scratch. For the best burger meat, source different cuts of beef from your butcher – don't just use ready-minced beef. The benefit of this is you know that you can cook a delicious medium-rare or, even better, a rare burger!

Ready-minced beef has to be cooked thoroughly if you do not know which part of the animal it has come from. The best mix of cuts for a really juicy and tasty burger is some lean meat off the bone and some with nice fatty bits – a good ratio is 20 per cent fat to 80 per cent meat.

MAKES 10 × 200G BURGERS

EQUIPMENT
Food processer (optional)
Griddle pan

1kg beef (mixed as above)
10 burger buns or English muffins
Olive oil
Sea salt and freshly ground black pepper

To serve
Cheese, sliced (optional)
Red onion, sliced
Gherkins
Pickles

You could have your butcher mince the meat for you, but if you are doing it yourself place your food-processor blade (and the bowl too, if it fits) in the freezer for 30 minutes. Chop the beef into 2cm chunks and put them on a tray in your freezer for about 20 minutes until they have hardened – but do not allow them to freeze. Pulse the chilled meat in batches until coarsely minced.

Fully chilled meat and fat will not split or partially cook from the heat generated while mincing in the food processor. The golden rule is not to overwork the meat and fat. Keep the minced meat in the fridge until you are ready to use it and do not season the meat until just before cooking as salt affects it, dissolving proteins and drawing out the moisture, resulting in a springy, sausage-like texture when it is cooked.

When you are ready to cook the burgers, preheat your griddle pan to a very high temperature.

Form the burgers into roughly 200g patties, trying not to overwork the meat or pack the mince too tightly. It depends on the size of your buns – we like to use English muffins – but make the patties slightly wider than the buns as they will shrink during cooking. After forming the patties, use your thumb to push a dimple into the top of each one, which stops them puffing up into a ball.

Once the pan is scorching hot, brush both sides of each burger with a little olive oil and season generously with sea salt and pepper. Place in the pan to cook, turning regularly. If you are very serious about how you like your meat done, a meat thermometer comes in extremely handy at this stage. A rough temperature guide for cooking is: 49–54°C for rare; 57–63°C for medium; 68°C and above for well done.

You need to insert the thermometer into the middle of the burger and remove the burger from the pan a few degrees before your desired temperature as it will continue to cook once it comes off the heat. If you want to melt cheese on top, do this on the last flip.

To serve, lightly toast or heat your burger buns or muffins and build your burger using sliced red onion and gherkins and, of course, whatever condiments you like.

Mushroom Ketchup (Gubbeen Worcestershire Sauce)

The story of the famous Lea & Perrin's Worcestershire sauce mentions the inventors' feeling of failure when they first tasted the barrels full of this type of 'ketchup' – but a year went by and it was re-sampled, and the rest is history! This sauce also benefits from a long rest on the shelf once made, so resist the temptation of using it too soon – 16 weeks is not too long.

MAKES 500–600ML

- 1.3kg mushrooms, peeled and chopped (field mushroom glut is ideal)
- 75g salt
- 150ml white wine vinegar
- 150ml balsamic vinegar (not an expensive version)
- 2 teaspoons diced shallots
- 1 teaspoon peppercorns
- 1 teaspoon allspice
- 2 blades of mace
- 2 teaspoons whole cloves
- 1 cinnamon stick
- 50ml brandy
- 50ml fino sherry
- 2 tablespoons cane sugar

Stir the prepared mushrooms and salt together in a large bowl. Leave, covered, for 2 days, squashing occasionally, encouraging the mushrooms to release their juices.

Put the mushrooms along with all the other ingredients into a large pan, bring to the boil, then simmer for 2 hours.

Strain the liquid through a sieve – for very clear sauce I suggest you line the sieve with a coffee filter.

Pour the ketchup into a sterilised bottle, seal and leave to mature in a cool, dark place for at least 16 weeks before use.

Oxtail with Bavarian Bread Dumplings

This is a rich and hearty dish – the juices from the oxtail make the gravy unique and if there is any left after your dinner on day one, you can certainly make a soup the following day when the richness will have done that wonderful 'next day' thing.

SERVES 6

1 tablespoon beef dripping
2.5kg oxtail, cut into chunks
12 round shallots
50g unsalted butter
2 large onions, sliced
12 garlic cloves
390g jar pickled walnuts, drained, vinegar reserved
300ml red wine
500ml stout
Salt and freshly ground black pepper

For the bread dumplings
250ml milk
1 teaspoon nutmeg, grated
5 or 6 white bread rolls
Knob of butter
1 free-range egg
4 shallots, finely chopped
40–50g parsley, stalks removed and finely chopped
Flour, for dusting
Salt and freshly ground black pepper

Preheat the oven to 130°C/gas mark 1. Select a large, flameproof casserole pot with a lid, one that can accommodate all the ingredients. Melt the dripping, season the chunks of oxtail and fry over a medium heat. Because the chunks of tail are all different knobbly shapes and sizes they demand a fair bit of attention and will need turning and moving around the pan until the fat is a satisfying golden colour and the meat is caramelised. Transfer the oxtail to a large bowl or pot and add the shallots to the casserole pot. Brown the shallots all over as best you can and put them in the bowl with the oxtail. Now add the butter, onions and garlic to the pot, turn the heat down a touch and cook with the lid on until soft.

When the onions are soft and yielding, add the drained vinegar from the jar of pickled walnuts, with the wine and stout. Bring to the boil, return the oxtail and shallots to the casserole, taste for seasoning, adding salt pinch by pinch as necessary, and a grind of pepper for good measure. Cover the pot and place in the oven for 4½ hours, or until the oxtail is completely tender.

Meanwhile, make the dumplings. Gently warm the milk in a saucepan and grate in the nutmeg. Roughly tear up the rolls into a large bowl and pour over the warmed milk. Let them soak for about 30 minutes or until well softened.

Sweat the shallots in the butter. Add the beaten egg, the sweated shallots and the chopped parsley to the softened rolls and season well. Mix everything together – it will be a moist consistency – and then, using wet hands, form the dumplings to roughly the size of golf balls. 20 mintues before the oxtail is cooked, remove the casserole from the oven and turn up the temperature to 220°C/gas mark 7. Place the dumplings on top of the stew (they will soak up all that lovely fat), brush the surfaces with the beaten egg and return the pot to the oven with the lid off. The dumplings are cooked when they resemble freshly baked bread. If you have extra dumplings and don't want to fill the stew pot entirely, bring a large pot of salty water to the boil, reduce to a gentle simmer (if it boils they will fall apart), carefully add the remaining dumplings, then simmer for 20 minutes. Gently remove from the water and let them sit for a while before frying in some butter.

Allow the stew to cool for 10–15 minutes and serve with mashed swede and the pickled walnuts.

Steak and Kidney Pie

That magic double act – steak and kidney – I don't think it ever went out of fashion, but if it did, try this once, and you will never be parted again! I remember my first great homemade steak and kidney experience: it was as a young girl at my best friend Penny's house, and when her Ma shook the cut meats together in a plastic bag full of flour and thyme, right there I knew something special was happening! It is this sort of home cooking that, like great friendships, stays with you all your life.

SERVES 4–6

For the pastry

100g self-raising flour
50g shredded suet (e.g. Atora)
1 teaspoon thyme leaves
4–5 tablespoons water
1 free-range egg, beaten
Salt and freshly ground black pepper

For the filling

700g lean beef stewing steak, cut into 2.5cm dice
2–3 tablespoons beef dripping, duck fat or olive oil
1 large onion, sliced
230g mushrooms, sliced
3 sprigs of thyme
30g butter
1 tablespoon flour
2 tablespoons Mushroom Ketchup (see page 39) or Worcestershire sauce
425ml beef or chicken stock
1 bay leaf
150g ox kidney, trimmed of sinew, cut into 1cm dice
Salt and freshly ground black pepper

To make the pastry, combine the flour and suet in a bowl, add the thyme and season. Make a well in the centre and add the water. Mix it all into a nice soft but not sticky dough. Cover the bowl and leave to rest in the fridge for at least 30 minutes.

For the filling, season the beef. Put 2 tablespoons of the dripping or oil in a large, heavy-based pan over a high heat and, in batches, fry the meat on all sides. When the cubes are browned, remove using a slotted spoon to a bowl and set aside.

Fry the onion with a pinch of salt in the same pan, picking up all that goodness at the bottom of the pan left behind by the meat. When the onion is softened, add the mushrooms and thyme sprigs and turn off the heat.

For the sauce we make a little roux. Start by frying the butter in a non-stick pan till it froths, whisk in the flour and cook together over a medium heat for a minute or two, stirring constantly. Whisk in the mushroom ketchup, then add the stock a little at a time. Once all the liquid is added, you should have tasty, lump-free gravy. Add your bay leaf to this.

Add the gravy and the beef to the pan with the onion and mushrooms and mix together. Taste for seasoning and acidity, adding a little more mushroom ketchup and salt if need be. Grind in some pepper, cover and stew over a low heat for about 2 hours. When your meat is tender, remove from the heat and allow to cool.

When you are ready to make the pie, preheat the oven to 180°C/gas mark 4.

Heat a little more dripping or olive oil in a pan over a high heat. Salt the kidney and fry in the very hot pan. You are not cooking the kidney at this stage, just giving it good colour, and it will really add to the flavour. Finally add the kidney to the stew.

Take the suet pastry out of the fridge – it will crack if it's too cold when you roll it out, although it shouldn't be too soft either or it will be difficult to handle!

Select your casserole dish (I use one that is 25cm wide and 12.5cm deep) and roll out the pastry to size, allowing about 1cm excess to seal round the rim of the dish. The pastry should be about 0.75cm thick.

Transfer all the filling ingredients to the casserole dish, brush the edges of the dish with some of the beaten egg, place the pastry over the top and pinch it to the rim to seal. Glaze the pastry with more egg and bake the pie in the oven for 25–30 minutes until the pastry is perfectly golden.

Brussels sprouts were always traditional with this pie, or you can serve it with kale and mashed potatoes.

Gentleman's Relish

This is a very versatile 'condiment'. It works wonderfully on the side with beef, chicken, pork and lamb. It's also perfect for dressings or slathered over some toasted sourdough with a boiled egg or two.

Please use the very best anchovies you can get your hands on. If you can't get decent ones it's not worth the effort of making this sauce.

MAKES A FULL 300ML KILNER JAR

EQUIPMENT
Stick blender

100g best-quality anchovies in oil (Ortez make a great choice)
1 garlic clove, minced
30ml water
175ml olive oil
2 teaspoons red wine vinegar

Tip the anchovies into the tall beaker that comes with your stick blender, including the oil from their tin or jar, then add the garlic.

Blitz the anchovies, jiggling the blender until you have a rough paste. Add the water to loosen the anchovies – again you will have to jiggle the blender, but don't lift it out of the beaker while blitzing or you'll end up with tiny dots of anchovy everywhere.

Add the olive oil, little by little, incorporating each amount fully before you add the next. Lastly blitz in the red wine vinegar. Transfer to a jar and cover.

The salt content of the anchovies will keep this relish in a fridge once opened for 2 weeks. If it is not opened, it will keep for a month.

The Sponge

There was a lot of tea when Tom was young – it came with aunts, visits from clergy, and the good china. This sponge calls for equal quantities of sugar, butter, flour and eggs. The easiest way to achieve this is to weigh the eggs, still in their shells, record that weight and weigh out your sugar, butter and flour accordingly.

SERVES A FAMILY

2 free-range eggs
Unsalted butter, softened
Caster sugar
Self-raising flour, sifted
1 teaspoon vanilla extract
Pinch of salt

Preheat the oven to 180°C/gas mark 4. Grease a 26cm tin with butter and line with greaseproof paper – make a circle for the base and trim the offcuts to line the sides.

Weigh the eggs in their shells, record the total weight and set aside. Weigh the same amount of butter.

Put the butter in a high-sided mixing bowl and cream with a wooden spoon until it becomes very soft. Weigh the same amount of caster sugar and mix it into the butter, a quarter at a time. Continue mixing until fluffy and light. Weigh out the same quantity of flour.

Crack the eggs into a jug and whisk. Beat the eggs into the sugar and butter little by little, incorporating fully each time. You run the risk of splitting the mix by adding too much egg at once. Add a tablespoon of the flour to the sugar and butter when you have a third of your egg left: this will help the last of the egg into the mix. Lastly add the vanilla extract along with the salt.

Sift the flour over the cake mixture and fold it in gently, this time using a tablespoon – the thinner edge of a metal spoon has less impact on the mix. A good technique is turning the bowl as you fold so you aren't just mixing in one spot. Check the consistency isn't too thick: it should 'drop' but not run off the spoon. (A tablespoon of milk can be added if the mixture is stiff.)

Pour the mixture into the prepared tin and bake in the oven for 25–30 minutes.

Stick a skewer into the middle of the cake: if the skewer comes out clean, the sponge is ready. By tapping the tin on your work surface you allow some of the steam inside the cake to be released and this helps prevent it sinking.

Rest the cake in the tin for 10 minutes, then remove from the tin and allow to cool completely on a rack.

Lovely whipped double cream and homemade jam were perfect fillings, as I remember, and they still are. You can also decorate the top of this cake with leaves or doillies as stencils, sifting icing sugar over them for patterns.

FORD

2

THE FARMYARD

THE foods that we make here in Gubbeen in one way or another all come from the farm. The mainstay of our family income had, for a long time, been the cheeses produced from our milk and the pigs reared and fed on some of the whey made during the cheese production. Now Clovisse, who over the years has fed us all with superb vegetables from her garden and grown the herbs that flavour Fingal's salami cures, has added another dimension – the Garden Lunches.

All this activity is centred on the farm and how it is run, guided and managed by Tom. Our home, like most West Cork farms, is based in the kitchen. This big, old, black-raftered room backs onto the pantry, which leads out of the half-door into the narrow path beside the dairy and up to the animals. This is the Haggard, the big yard where the young animals are fed and cared for, where the straw is stored, where the sows have their bonhams (Irish for piglets) and also where the herd's maternity shed is watched over. It is not only the oldest part of the farm but the hub of Tom's work. We have old sepia photographs of Tom's father and uncles as boys that show it pretty much as it is now; some trees have gone, and the sheds are bigger now, but even back then the Haggard was centre stage.

In our generation the surrounding sheds have grown in size as a result of the progression Tom oversaw from milk production to cheese production. The herringbone milking parlour where, every morning and evening at 6, our herd comes in to be milked is our second since the decision to move out of the pipeline system of Tom's youth. The current parlour, with its 10-a-side milking bays arranged fishbone fashion, is painted rather a good shade of sky blue, as a report we read many years ago suggested it disoriented flies!

The distinctive hum as the vacuum starts in the morning is strangely peaceful. Like all the work done with cattle, there is a certain slow pace that the animals need. In the evenings, as the motor stops, a stillness comes over the yard, the calves are fed and, as dusk falls, it's down time. Behind the parlour is the bulk-tank area, the big storage tanks where the milk is chilled and where the cooler pipes and the washers are located. It's from here that the milk starts its journey, piped through a small hole in the wall into the cheese dairy.

The Haggard is dominated these days by the big over-wintering house we call the Big Shed. This is home to the dairy herd during the winter and its sturdy design has been well tested by the gales and the storms that hit it, almost uninhibited by any windbreak, straight off the Atlantic. In here the cows have rather a high-tech winter existence. They wear earring transponders, which are linked to Fingal's

computer. The data it holds on each cow's milk volume and gestation point determines how much feed is doled out automatically to each cow from the feed stations that run down the centre of the shed. I have a feeling, though, that Tom has it all in his head!

What I particularly like about this system is that the big old greedy galleons – usually the Friesians – in an uncontrolled free-for-all would shoulder the little Jersey girls or the light Kerry cows out of the way to hog all the ration, but here they are foiled. They put their heads into the feeder and if the transponder reads them as having had their allowance for the day, no feed is let down and they shuffle off. I would probably buy a fridge that worked on this principle but whether teenagers could be talked into wearing transponders is another matter! The over-wintering shed is smart in other ways, too. A long tram track runs down each side of the cows' beds in which a cleaning system slowly and regularly pushes the slurry down to the holding tanks under slats at the end of the shed. So the herd is warm, clean and properly fed over winter, one and all.

Backing onto this shed are our silage pits. It takes long hours of harvesting all through the summer months to fill these up, then they sit fermenting into autumn covered in black plastic and tyres like huge sauerkraut vessels. We have a system for draining the grass juices off these pits that Tom calls the Cocktail Bar – a channel leads to a pipe that directs the juices down into the parlour yard to drip quietly into a trough. These juices are slightly fermented (and I would guess slightly alcoholic) with rather a good, sweet smell, which brings a few very determined cows to get their noses into the trough, returning again and again with big, moist-eyed excitement written on their faces.

Off the back end of the Haggard, beside the tall feed bins that have a strange Cape Canaveral look to them, is the Old Big Shed. This is where 'shed-life' goes on. It is the best place on earth for children: Tom has seen three generations grow up in there. It was where he and his sister Carol used to plot to catch the yard cats and coral then in the wheelbarrow with a net on top – Carol still has scars. It was where Clovisse would guzzle calf nuts before coming in to her dinner and worrying me sick with her non-eating. It was where Fingal fell in love with knives and blew himself up, twice, and where unknown mischief and experiments go on. These days our grandsons Olan and Oscar spend hours in there, catching small piglets.

All the young animals live in this shed, along with my flock of layers whose house backs onto the old orchard. The poultry vie with the weaning piglets for who can make the most noise, with the cockerels winning in the morning and the weaners at tea time as they squabble over the feed. This shed is also the farrowing area, housing the sows about to farrow, and those that already have their litters. The noise they make as they warp and grunt to feed the newborn bonhams is probably the most ancient sound I know.

Off one end is a long barn, home to the weaned piglets as they grow on in a progression of big, airy, straw-filled pens with feeders and water on permanent access. An entire side of this area can be opened to the air by means of huge, garage-type doors that are lifted up on calm days when there is no westerly blowing in. Our young pigs quite possibly contemplate some of the best real-estate views in West Cork: across the sea, down over the islands and out to Fastnet.

In the middle of this shed is the straw – baled and stacked high for the winter; by spring the stack has dwindled to a pile to be eked out until the animals can go back out to the pasture. When city friends ask if their children can come and spend time with ours in this noisy, smelly, primordial 'paradise', there is the moment of concern. All life goes on here: birth, sex, death and tragedies, little runts who don't make the struggle to their mothers' teats, cats guzzling my chicks, or the brutal bullying that will suddenly break out in the young weaners. Strangely enough, children accept this. For some people, perhaps through generations of separation from the land, there is an anxiety. Have we been too over-sensitised with anti-bacterial wipes and Bambi to understand any more the mud and gutters of the farmyard? Will Health & Safety turn these old yards into HACCP and risk-assessed areas – nature red in tooth and

claw brought in to heel by EU regulations and hygiene fears?

Beside the Old Big Shed is the maternity ward for the cattle where the young calves are born, and opposite is where they are fed for the first few weeks of life, and then in winter where they grow on in straw and where they live in summer before they leave to go out to pasture. In this part of the shed are the smells of sweet calf milk – beestings or colostrum – and the rich, milky breath of the little calves themselves. Housed in cubicles filled with bedding straw and suckling buckets, they are nursed along by the skills and constant attention of Andrew Brennan, a very observant and dedicated carer.

Our herd is made up of many breeds for the cheese: Friesian, Simmental, Shorthorn, Jersey and Ireland's own little black Kerry cows all have their calves here and the nursery is a serious place with huge responsibilities and much hard work to keep them well and thriving. Not just once a month but each and every day, morning and evening, and all the in-between times. Calf-rearing needs a very special character: patient, observant, kind and with a very strong back – you spend hours teaching the little ones to suckle with your head at knee height! I am not too sure that European regulations haven't rather spoiled the looks of lovely little calves. These days each calf born has to have its health and movement status, along with its ID and breeding, follow it from birth to death. This is done by large yellow tags with barcodes carrying its individual numbers and information on both ears, front and back. On newborns they seem ridiculous, dragging their ears down to a woeful angle that gives them a forlorn look, another little bit of eurocracy they have to grin and bear.

So here in the heart of the farm is the beginning of the Food Story. The milk from the cows, the birth and nurture of the pigs and calves and the hens that lay for us the free-range eggs we sell at the markets. From here the animals and the foods as raw materials fan out along their routes to either the cheese dairy or the smokehouse. It's also from here that the composted dungs are carried back onto our land, to complete the cycle of land to food and back to land.

The whole day over, from Tom turning on the milking machine first thing in the morning, until the last of the fowl has been rounded up into its fox-safe shed, and the last calf has been fed and the pigs are strawed and reshuffled, when even the nosy peacock who seems to patrol us knowingly all day finally flies up onto the roof beam, it's then that Tom or Andrew will turn off the lights and the farmyard goes quiet and feral and private.

HOWARD

The Yard Birds

GEESE

It was stepping into big shoes when we started rearing geese again at Gubbeen. Tom's grandmother had always kept and fattened geese, not only hatched and reared them, but plucked and separated the down from the feathers for the eiderdowns and pillows here, stuffing the old flour sacks that were made from such good-quality linen. She used every single piece of the birds: necks, gizzards, livers of course; also the beautiful wings were dried off as the best brushes for the Aga and the grates, and the children were given the windpipes to blow like whistles that let out the goose call! In all innocence I had no idea what a world of work I had taken on.

Geese are complicated and determined birds. I had heard all the stories of how Tim's grandmother had to separate the geese once they laid as they took each other's eggs, how she managed their housing once the goslings had hatched, fattened them on potatoes and parata (flaked maize) and how, with her care and never-ending watchfulness for 'Mr Reynard', she got them to the Christmas table. It sounded to me like a major labour of love, both for the family and the animals.

We favour American Buff geese, with their large bodies and orange beaks and legs. By December they can weigh in live at 22–25lb (10–11kg). The old gander had a lovely trait of going grey around his beak as he aged. Once I had mastered the game of not threatening him by coming between him and his young or, worst of all, pointing at him which brought on the clatter of paddles and terrifying escaping gas noises as he charged, no doubt thinking my pointing finger was a beak and my arm a neck, we made a sort of suspicious pact: I would feed him and his family and once a year he would feed mine.

My plan was to incubate eggs I would pirate from the laying geese in the spring (so they wouldn't compete over nests), hatch them, then brood them on and finally somehow introduce them back to their parents. My early incubator had no mechanics: I was turning the eggs by hand at least five times a day. I managed to steal the eggs from the geese when the gander was not looking, and the hatch was progressing well. At 20 days you could hear the pipping, then a crack, then the tiny beak broke through. Some part of me knew that if you could hold off helping them out of the eggs, you would be passing some significant test. It is one of the hardest things not to crack off bits of the shell to try to help their passage into our world from their eggness. The sad truth, though, is that if they are not strong enough to make it out of the egg, they certainly won't make it through Yard Life, but happily a good few always do.

Newborn goslings are actually pale green and they are everything Walt Disney is all about: sweet, innocent and vulnerable. It was love! Two memories always come back to me when I see goslings. One was my first glimpse of my father-in-law Willie, as he came wandering up the avenue with a little vapour trail of smoke coming out of his pipe, a gosling and a lamb trotting after him. He'd taken these orphans and fed them, and they had imprinted on him; he was 'Mama'. The other was an old teacher who criticised my brother who wanted to leave school early to travel: 'He's green as a Devonshire gosling,' he warned my mother! He was, too, but like the goslings he was determined.

Goslings make their presence intensely felt from day one, roaring for food, water and grass and growing so fast that having them under the hot lamp for warmth became a challenge of hooks and pulleys. They have to be taken out at least twice a day for a swim, first in the sink, then in

a paddling pool to develop their legs. Those huge paddles and wobbly limbs will need to hold up a serious body weight, so getting them strong in the first weeks is a pretty important challenge and swimming is gosling Pilates.

Most years there will be at least four of these needy green toddlers, always hungry and tightly bonded to their handler. For several months after they hatch you can't walk the yard in a straight line as they wind themselves between your feet. When the timing works and the hatching of the parent geese brood coincides with that of our incubator family, you only have to wait and subtly introduce them daily on their walkabouts, bringing them closer and closer to the geese. At first the adults charge them as aliens, then one day they decide they are theirs and confidently lure them off to graze; the goslings too know this is for them and, with no backward glance, they go. It's a great sense of a job well done when this happens, the cavalry has arrived and you can retire.

All summer long as the geese do their march past they really touch you, that troupe arrangement geese have, big gander out front, then a female with the goslings safe in the middle followed up by another female. They are just wonderful parents, incredibly calm, caring and watchful. They slowly parade their young off to sweet open grass patches, then sit and watch, one eye facing north, one south, the other parent at an opposite angle, covering east and west, really alert for any attack with their beady dark hazel eyes, but still and calm and comforting, egging on their young to graze.

POULTRY

My first hen was a birthday present from Tom. She was an Andalusian, a lovely little black hen with large white ear lobs. She laid perfect white eggs, now and then. We had always kept layers, that rather sad, rusty, non-breed that had laying characteristics tweaked up until they became rather simple and short-lived bumblers that simply ate, slept and laid.

This slick black hen moved into the hen run and stood out in so many ways it was impossible not to fall for pure-breeds. She immediately became top dog, fed first, slept on the highest rung, called in a strong soprano voice when she had laid – not a common event, but I would fly in to see this marvellous white egg, which was put into a box alongside the poor old layers' dismal offerings of uniform tinted ovals: it stood out, just as she did.

Thereafter the hunt was on. I had to find other breeds of hen that laid such beautiful eggs, ones that carried genes that have been around for as long as man has been enclosing land to survive. I knew they were out there, so I could dream and plan. I had the vision of egg boxes full of all these coloured eggs, white, dark brown, speckled and even blue – I'd heard a rumour I didn't quite believe of blue eggs. How beautiful and how addictive this hen breeding was to become.

As I hunted down breeders at the Cork agricultural shows I kept hearing one name again and again, Willie Evans. He had bred pure lines of some of the more stunning chickens for years, dedicating his life to learning about fowl, their lines, their plumage and the standards they should be bred to. By sheer luck he lived nearby and once I had accounted for myself and convinced him that I knew what I was doing (very important when you are breeding rare and valuable animals), he let me have eggs to hatch and soon my flock grew in quality. Thanks to Willie's suggestions and having seen his really good birds, I started to get my eye in and by the 90s I had around ten breeds. Our garden started to look like a shanty town, erratic housing spreading across the lawns. In the spring I would oversee this rather tough eugenics programme with cocks and hens running together in threesomes to give me fertile eggs for the incubators, which by this time had been upgraded to smart, self-turning, temperature- and humidity-controlled machines – with far better results. Poor Tom, even his dining room table had chicks brooding on it: he was married to a woman obsessed!

Hens, like geese, will imprint up to a point, but it is their pecking order that fascinates me. They live in linear social hierarchies; they know who is stronger and who is weaker. The flock is a complex and very interesting social group, not

unlike traditional societies in which there are natural leaders and followers, the hunters and the gatherers and the warm cosy ones who have lots of chicks!

The cockerels for all their posing are diligent patriarchs calling the hens to feed and breaking up hen fights with a flourish of wings and a charge. I find hens rather cunning, but intelligent. Their knowledge of predators and where to find food makes them very interesting, good companions for gardeners, if you don't mind their dust-bath habits always being in the driest borders or your newly raked salad patch.

You can become really very attached to hens, and there are some individual ones whom I'm afraid we do call by name. They have serious roles to play in our yard and they are mourned when they go. There were several horror stories and I still quake at the memory of a mink attack. Like all predators and bullies it had hunted for our weakness, it had found a tiny break in the wire and went about its vile bloodthirsty work, killing over 30 hens, making dreadful wounds in their necks. As Tom headed off to the burial grounds with a wheelbarrow full of these still-warm corpses, I dealt with my emotions as best I could, the guilt, the fury, the sense of loss, but above all, and most worrying, was my sinister longing for revenge.

There is no sleepless night like that of the farmer who wakes, knowing there is a fox or mink creeping into the yard. Your ears become like some distant ancestor's, catching every leaf moving, scanning for what could be a hen calling. If there is a predator in the garden and Tom makes it downstairs to the gun and over to the window or door in time, the staggering noise of a shot in the night is so dreadful it cancels all thoughts of vengeance – all you guiltily hope for is a clean kill! I soon found some balance from that old contract all farmers have with predators, and I still hold that there is justice in an eye for an eye and a beak for a beak.

It might have been the losses to fox and mink that wore me down or perhaps it was maturity that brought me to just one breed, but the absolute stars of the hen world for me are Brahmas. These are the gentle giants of our Gubbeen yard. They are huge, beetle-browed, soft-feathered and have knickerbocker legs. The cocks walk like Greek soldiers, tossing their legs forward, heads up and shoulders back. They were raised to nobility status by Queen Victoria – whom they strongly resemble. She was given nine birds from Brahmaputra, which she bred on and then popularised.

I started with blues, some of whose feathers are laced with a lighter grey, which somehow makes them look even bigger and softer than the golden girls. I paired them in that magical match of gold cockerel to pure grey hen. This combination produces the Partridge Brahma. What a stunner, with pale grey undercoat and gold laced on top, it looks *so* well dressed.

Now each year brings me single-minded and determined to the incubator with these lines I have been nursing along for quite some time now, and each year two or three pure grey and buff Partridge Brahmas are lavished with admiration, food and pretty much the run of the yard. It is still a thrill to watch the eggs break open and to see the pale chick with the little dark lines that will, come autumn, develop into lovely plumage. If I am honest, though, it has to be said that they have a fatal flaw: they lay one of the smallest eggs of all the soft-feathered breeds, but it rather touches me that they are not perfect!

NEXT
DENIM

Chicken Housing and Feed

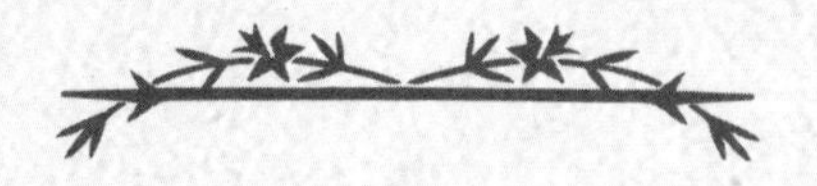

Keeping chickens is largely a question of common sense and sympathy. If you like these birds your instincts will be to keep them dry, well fed and not too crowded, which is of course the best way to rear them! As we have a large haggard (farmyard) where the chickens can freely peck and scratch in safety from foxes, with a gate that leads down to the orchard, the licence that we hold for the sale of eggs at the farmers' markets puts us in the 'free range' category.

Having birds out on grass and, if at all possible, ranging freely over quite a wide area, say in an old orchard or wild part of a garden, where they can scratch for worms and bugs under dry leaves is perfect. Personally, I love seeing the birds down in our garden, but they have a terrible habit of digging dust-baths for themselves and always choose the warmest and best soil – in other words bang in the middle of your border where you have just sown your summer annuals or transplanted your lettuce seedlings.

Chickens have the same tendencies as some teenagers: you encourage them to eat well and sleep in tidy rooms, but 10 minutes after you have tidied up after them, the whole area is like a war zone. I am now more inclined to leave them to do what they want all day and simply manage their night times carefully. (The chickens, that is; teenagers are another matter…)

So, from my knowledge of chickens, the best advice I can offer, based on the way we manage our flocks, is this:

Floor space: You will need a dry, airy but warm area that can house nine hens per square metre of floor space.

Floor cover: The floor should be covered with either straw or wood shavings, but as the straw can be streeled out onto the grass or surrounding area by the birds' claws, which can look messy I prefer to use wood shavings during the dry summer days. In the wet of winter, however, I go for straw as it is warmer and mops up the wet the birds haul in from foraging outside. There is now a lovely product, Miscanthus or Elephant Grass, which is perfect for all seasons.

Neutralising bedding powder: I mix a dusting of a white chalky powder called Sanitise with the straw. This is a bedding conditioner made by Agritech – there are various alternatives. Its chalky base, with perhaps some lime for hygiene, cleans and absorbs and it has a strong peppermint smell – good for repelling mites.

Ranging area: EU rules give a figure of 1,000 hens per acre. As we have never dreamt of having such a huge flock, all I can say is that fowl will scratch and dig up beautiful green grassy pasture just before it rains, and then dance it into a muddy mess faster than you can manage to rotate them, so the bigger the area, the better. The absolutely best design is to have a central house with the land around it fenced; you rotate in a circular fashion, moving the internal fence around the 'clock face' one quarter hour at a time to allow the grass to regrow.

Perching: It is really important that birds can perch, both for the health of their feet (walking all day splays their claws and gripping a perch at night keeps them strong), and for their general wellbeing – it is a deeply ingrained instinct for hens to fly up at night to perch. The perch needs to allow each hen 15cm, no less – on warm nights under a thin roof they can get very hot. I love to see them in winter, huddled together for warmth.

Water: A good supply of clean water is vital. Hens drink far more than you might imagine; they are 70 per cent water and hold it in their body tissue. What they eat and how well they are laying determine the amount of water they need. This is something you need to take into account when deciding what to feed them: molasses and some soya feeds, both high in magnesium, would not be good for poultry as the mineral content would, like salt, have to be excreted. Consequently they would need a higher water intake so that the minerals did not build up in the birds' kidneys. Temperature, of course, will affect how much water hens need – they will drink twice as much at 30°C as at 15°C. Hens pant if they are too warm and generally don't thrive unless they have lots of water to replace this moisture loss.

Immediately they have laid an egg, hens are inclined to go straight for a drink to replace the lost moisture and at night, just before they perch, they go to the water trough. If there is no fresh water, birds will stop eating, they will not lay and generally go on strike, so permanent clean fresh water is really key to success. The best system is a constant water supply with a ballcock system that you keep a good eye on, and a trough you can clear out every two or three days as they fill it up with food and debris backwash. I always use small (2–5-litre hand-held) metal water containers to be sure that the hens are used to them; if I need to give them a remedy or worm them, I mix the medication in these containers, so it is vital they are accustomed to them.

If the container is the only source of water, and you find it empty each day as you go to refill it, you are certainly not giving them enough water – buy a second container.

Worms and other ailments: I use a herbal system called Vermex – it also acts as a tonic and, if you are inclined to keep a record of the number of eggs you are getting, just for fun see whether the count goes up a few days after the Vermex dose – I have noticed that it does. (You would not give this medication permanently as its herbal content works to shock the system and get rid of the worms. Every month for five days I include it in the water source, following the manufacturer's instructions.)

Often – at least once a week while they are laying – I put organic cider vinegar in the hens' water trough (a teaspoon per litre a day is fine) and a slice of garlic too as it repels or certainly supports low worm infestation

Sadly, we no longer have poultry instructors whom you can contact if there is a health problem. Each year I test our bedding and floor droppings for salmonella, which is easy for us as we do bacterial testing every week, but there are labs in all areas who will do this for you – it's worth it for peace of mind and you will not worry about any dirt on the eggshells. Mites are manageable with good mite powders and clean housing. Once any illness presents itself, however, I would always seek professional help. Things spread so quickly with fowl and they can be easy to nip in the bud with good advice and hygiene – but do remember, if you are given antibiotics or complex medication, not to use the eggs until the withdrawal period has ended.

Nesting: For every seven hens EU regulations require you to provide a nest box measuring 45 × 45cm. I dutifully bought two rather fine banks of six nesting boxes with removable trays for the hens to lay in – the eggs roll into the trough at the front for ease of collection. I do get eggs in this beautiful system, but it is the old wine box on the floor where they prefer to lay!

The regulations also require anyone selling eggs at markets to label the boxes with their address and contact details, but this applies only if your flock numbers 50 birds or more.

Feed: There is one rule here – the very best you can afford. Nutrition for layers is complex and detailed, so do buy layers' mash or pellets rather than just throwing them scraps and a handful of grain – you will be amazed at how the egg numbers grow if your birds are really well fed. If you can stretch to it, feed that is both organic and produced professionally for layers is really great, and it will give you and your flock the very best health benefits. Perhaps buy it once a month and bulk it up with rolled oats or barley. I sometimes remember to add linseed, which the hens just love, and it's worth the extra cost as it adds omega-3 to the eggs. During winter, when there are no offcuts from the vegetable garden, I do try to find an old cabbage or some carrot tops for them. Luckily, they love the last bits from the bottom of the drained cheese vat. It is hugely nutritious and they get all skittish about it. Now and then they get to drink some whey too – it's full of minerals that helps their feather growth.

TURKEYS

It took a while to form a friendship with our turkey cock. He permanently squared up to anyone who passed and had the charm of an unfriendly bouncer in a very successful nightclub.

You never felt welcome near him: the permanent bristling of his fan tail, the grinding of the strong wing feathers along the cement and those untrusting little beady eyes could unnerve. He didn't treat his women too well either. Apparently it is the turkey way to 'tread' his women to fertilise their eggs. You would come up the yard and find these rather stunned and flattened-looking females spread in a heap near the shed and there he would be with a self-satisfied, puffed-out chest.

As our male grew older, though, he got a name – George Bush. This helped, and his display too made him strangely less of a crank and more of an artist. If you ever happen to have time to spare and are near a turkey male, it is well worth watching his display. It is slow and really rather subtle. The wattle and snood – the long pendulous nose arrangement that hangs over the beak – along with the caruncles that are those corn-rows of bubbled flesh along the side of the neck and head, all very quietly change colour, from red to blue and then white. Unless you are watching carefully this *aurora borealis* effect can simply go unnoticed, so sit and observe closely to share his rather amazing little private light show.

You can also fool turkeys into making their mad call if you hum and simultaneously whistle at them. This triggers their head jerking and gobbling performance, which really is rather nice to experience – they put their all into it and look exhausted if you keep it up for too long!

This year I noticed George has developed a slight roll and was not pulling off his turns that used to be crisp and bang-on as you circled him; he used to be there with his eyes on you in a second, and now he seemed to be creaking. Giving him the once-over we discovered he has 'bumble foot', a swelling of the toes with sore lesions on the underfoot. We treated it, but with all that grumping about he had picked up a nasty infection that has left him with what looks rather like a bunion, all very in character, so George is now a senior citizen and would certainly wear a handkerchief with a knot at each corner if he were a human and lived by the coast. He had to endure two new males coming into the farm, which he pulled off really well and still holds a dignified position around the yards.

I do wonder how turkeys survived the wild; they have so little imagination and are such solid types. I once saw some in a wood in Paxos, one of the Greek islands off Corfu, smaller and leaner than domesticated breeds but noisy and with no subtlety, nor apparently capable of much flight. Maybe, though, they have a sacrificial survival game plan: they taste so delicious (at least, free-range ones reared on natural foods do) that they have become human pets and we their guardians – at least until Christmas.

Turkeys do lay the most beautiful eggs, almost conical, and the shells are as tough as nails. The little turkey poults arrive with a small drill-like tip on their beaks that they need to beat their way out of their incubation. Come to think of it, perhaps this accounts for their attitude – they arrive in the world having had to beat their way out of an extremely hard-shelled egg. Life is tough business, right?

Piglets/Bonhams

The hens don't get it all their own way in the yard. Andrew and I have a stand-off each month, as he quite rightly believes that the bonhams need to learn from the earliest days to fend for themselves and rifle around looking for food beyond their mother. He has devised a little trapdoor so they can sneak out of the farrowing pen and then head into the shed. Once they have braved the shed they edge further and further until they make it out to the yard. The piglets are usually about 10 days old when they meet their first hen and their political life begins.

The Brahma hens work the duchess routine – stunned by the vulgarity of the little pigs who bolt up to them then, like hipsters, pose and pout a little before doing cool turns and racing off back to the shed, they pretend nothing has happened. The Brahmas keep their heads up and rise above the whole encounter, but not for long. By two weeks old the piglets are working a tag team, bolting around and pushing their boundaries one after another – like kids on skateboards they skim the old hens, who bluster but give way.

It's not long before the bonhams find the orchard gate and then soon make headway down as far as the garden where the havoc of worm hunting begins. Here, my nerve gives out and I'm on to them, and Andrew has them moved into the straw-filled pens. Then the Brahmas are back running their own show for a week or two until another little black or pink snout makes it to the yard entrance.

The youngsters' only complete failure, as far as torturing feathered yard life goes, is the Bronze turkey cock. They charge him and do what piglets do, leaping back and forth to try to baffle him, but he is descended from Samurai. He stands and he stands, he grinds his tough wing feathers along the ground and lets off little explosions from somewhere in his puffed-up breast, the noise perfectly catching just how preposterous a piglet is, and to date I have never seen him give an inch. No matter how smart pigs are – and they are – it is the turkey cock, who knows who he is, who wins.

Rearing Pigs and Piglets

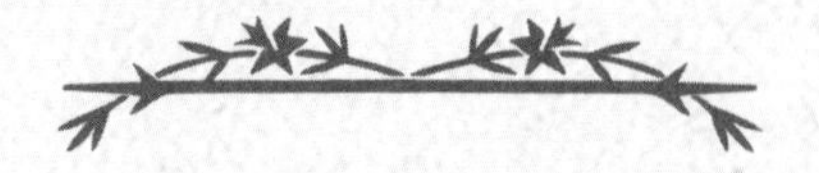

Andrew Brennan and Rosie Gingell have been the skilled and careful minders of our calves and pigs for many years. Rearing young animals well really is always about the personal commitment of the people who mind them.

The gestation of a pig is 3 months, 3 weeks and 3 days, like clockwork. Within 3 days of weaning and moving away from her litter at around 8 weeks, a sow will always come into heat again straight away. It does seem that nature has designed her to breed constantly. This might need careful managing if you run your boar with the sows.

A sow can have between 3 and 16 piglets, the size of her litter determined by a number of factors: fertility, age, breed, feed and general health. The first litter is usually a medium tidy 8, and subsequent litters seem to grow as the sow ages, until at around 5 years old she will start to produce smaller litters again.

We bring a sow in to farrow when we see signs of milk in the udder or if she is 'nesting'. With a lot of sows to watch, it is a good idea to keep careful notes too. Once in the farrowing house, which is warm, clean and fairly small, the sow will settle and usually within 6–10 hours of labour she will have her bonhams lined up under the hot lamp. We need to be very vigilant during this time – the mother needs peace and quiet, so dogs and other pigs are kept away, as understandably she might not be in very good humour. The bonhams need to suckle as soon as possible after birth, then every 3 hours for the first 24 hours. A healthy newborn bonham is blind and finds its way round to the teats by instinct within the first 3 hours – so they need a lot of minding at this point to help the weaker ones to feed if they get lost or if stronger ones push them off a teat. The sows' feed is carefully managed at this time, and they are fed a higher energy ration as soon as they come in to give birth and right on through until the young are weaned.

The piglets spend two weeks with their mother in the farrowing house, with a heat lamp for the young. For the first few days they are so thin-skinned and vulnerable they need a controlled environment of a heated space in close proximity to the sow. This space needs to be carefully designed as they could easily get lost in deep straw. Their key needs are to be kept dry and warm and near the sow. They become independent pretty quickly and by four days, being naturally inquisitive, they are happy to explore their environment and start to move out carefully into the wider world – we have a little hatch designed for them so they can get into the shed outside.

Pigs are highly intelligent animals and can recognise up to 30 faces – they certainly know people as individuals. Human contact is good, they look us in the eye, and relate to what we

are doing around them. So once or twice daily they really do need to be checked and share some contact with us. We get them fresh straw every day, which means they have housekeeping chores to do – they'll go and make up their beds and play areas, and always they have their own designated area for a WC which needs cleaning.

We indulge our pigs by swapping their pens too, which stops them getting bored with their environment. We hang heavy chains in their pens for them to play with, and other toys like footballs and even a big sack of used Sunday papers. Good friends from the village, one of whom used to work in Fleet Street and who still reads every newspaper printed on a Sunday, bring up this huge haul for the pigs. The literary supplements are flung into air, caught and shredded, the beauty magazines get pulled apart in a tug of war, and, shamefully, the editorials often end up trampled into the mire. It may sound fanciful, but if pigs get bored, they can start to pick on each other. You do need to know their calls and to react if you hear something going on as agitated pigs can do real damage to the others very fast. It is important to remember that while a bonham is one of the sweetest of all the farm young, small and bidable, a 5-year-old sow is the size of a sofa with a personality all of her own. We do try to rear them to be hardy, not dependent. There is a pride to a pig.

Our pens have one whole side that opens out to the fields and down to the sea. Pigs can, and do, watch the land and like the contact with the outside world. One thing pigs hate, though, is getting wet – they will always choose to be out of the rain if they have a chance, and with clean, airy pens and enough contact and distractions they can be easily managed to grow and thrive.

Notes on Caring for Calves

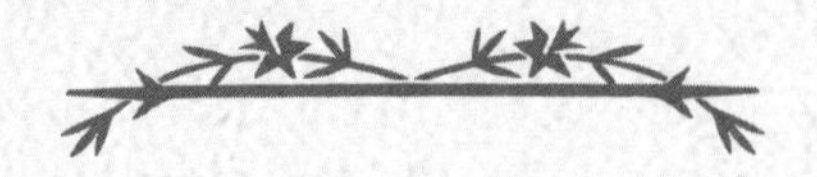

Andrew and Rosie manage the calving and the piglets. These are their insights.

We milk usually around 125 cows at Gubbeen. As our farm is based on cheesemaking, we calve all year round to guarantee the specialised milk production for the cheeses – a balanced protein and butterfat is best for us. Most dairy farms would calve in the autumn so their herds can graze the summer pasture then come in to calve as the weather closes in, drying them off (allowing them to stop producing milk) and housing them into the winter.

So we work off a calving calendar. Cattle gestate for 285 days, similar to humans. About two months before they are due, we dry them off and then about a week before their due date they arrive into our maternity ward, a field close to the yard in summer or, in winter, a straw-filled pen. Here they are watched carefully until they go into labour. It is not always one calf per cow; there can be twins or you can lose the odd calf, but of course most survive and are looked after carefully in our calving shed.

Once born, the young stay with their mother for the first couple of feeds of colostrum or, as it is called here, beestings. Colostrum is that first rich, highly nutritious milk the mother produces. It is very high in protein and full of antibodies – vital to establish a healthy immune system in newborns.

After two days with their mother the calves are moved into our calf world. Here the key management game for their welfare is their environment, so we keep them dry, with plenty of fresh air circulating around them. Our main worries while they are so young and vulnerable are viral – either pneumonias or intestinal scours. All newborns are carefully watched during this time. Our calving pens are designed with a slightly raised bedding area and draining flooring, all straw-filled. Attached to the doors are bucket holders for their drinking and feeding routine as they grow. They are fed twice a day, morning and evening.

We handle our animals quite a lot throughout their time as calves, to be sure they are well, and to train them to feed from the bucket. One of us goes into the pen with them to support their suckling by coaxing them to drink the warm milk. Whoever is milking will keep the newly calved cows' milk separate. It is drawn off the milking system into separate buckets for us to collect and take back to the calving pens to feed to the newborns. This handling encourages more settled and confident calves, so they learn to view humans as friendly and as a source of food – this

gives them confidence in us and they grow into calm animals. By the fourth day they are stronger, less sleepy and can start to take any cow's milk.

Our calves will stay in these pens and be fed milk twice a day for a week or so. During this time we slowly start them on calf nuts to supplement their milk and to get them used to solids. Gradually we change the diet system so that they are eating more and more solids. By the time they are about four months old they are moved into the larger calf pens outside in the main shed, growing on until they are ready to graze. In the warm summer months they go straight out to grass.

Easter Fairy Eggs

The best fun for imaginative children as this can make the egg shells look as if they were laid by fairy hens! Warning: when you hide eggs in the garden, do remember to shut your dog in so you don't suffer the unfortunate consequences that I experienced when my collie Hecate followed me around and ate them all before the children came out to go hunting!

MAKES 6 FAIRY EGGS

EQUIPMENT

6 × 25cm squares old sheet or cheesecloth
String

6 white-shelled free-range eggs
Outer skins from 1kg brown onions
Daisies or tiny Heartsease or Speedwell flowers

Lay the sheet or cheesecloth on the palm of your hand and place several overlapping layers of onion skin on top, then randomly place tiny flowers, such as daisy, speedwell or heartsease. Put a white egg on top and fold the combination halfway around the egg. Place more tiny flowers and onion skin on top of the egg so it is completely enveloped.

Carefully but firmly tie the egg up in a tiny bundle with the string. Repeat with the other eggs. Boil a pot of water and simmer gently for 15 minutes.

When the eggs have cooled, remove the shells and the magic is done. Once the fairy eggs have dried out they will last for the whole year.

The Best Scrambled Eggs

We enjoy this on Christmas Day with smoked salmon. Have your wooden spoon at hand – it only takes a minute or two and the eggs can stick if you are not ready to go as soon as the butter is hot. The secret is to use lots of butter. Crème fraîche is optional but delicious! Obviously, use fresh free-range eggs.

SERVES 2

4 thick slices of sourdough
4 free-range eggs
20g unsalted butter
1 tablespoon chopped chives
1 teaspoon crème fraîche (optional)
Salt and freshly ground black pepper

First toast your sourdough and keep it warm.

Crack the eggs into a jug and beat well. Melt the butter over a medium-high heat. When the butter starts to froth and bubble, add the eggs and remove the pan from the heat. Stir immediately, moving the spoon round the bottom and edges; there will be enough residual heat in the pan to cook the eggs to a silky-smooth consistency.

Add the chives and the crème fraîche (if using), mix, season and serve on your toasted sourdough.

Eggs in Hell

This is for a late breakfast. It is filling, totally satisfying and an excuse for adults to use the bread cut into soldiers. It's also a perfect 'morning after' food, as the fiery little peppers in the butter work miracles. Of course you can use hen eggs – fresh, free-range hen eggs are terrific – but the duck does produce a totally superior egg, creamy and richer and always that wonderful deep golden-orange yolk.

SERVES 1

1 duck egg
1 slice of sourdough
1 tablespoon crème fraîche
1 tablespoon Greek yogurt
1 chilli, chopped (Clovisse suggests jalapeño)
20g butter
Salt and freshly ground black pepper

First poach your duck egg in 1cm of rolling boil water, spooning the hot water over the yolk so that all the white is cooked around the yolk. Toast a slice of sourdough bread under the grill.

Combine the crème fraîche and yogurt in a bowl and warm the mixture by setting the bowl over a pan of nearly boiling water.

Melt the butter over a low heat, add the the chilli and lightly fry.

When the yogurt mixture is warm, transfer it to a warm serving plate or bowl and place the egg on top. Finish by pouring the chilli and butter over the egg. Dig in with the toast.

Egg and Cress Salad or Sandwiches

The salty capers and anchovies complement the eggs so well, but there is also a nice peppery addition from the cress. I like to have this on its own as a salad; however, a delicious sandwich can also be made by tossing the whole salad together before sandwiching it between slices of bread. I recommend a lovely fresh-baked white bread for the perfect comfort-food sandwich.

SERVES 4

100g American landcress or watercress, rinsed and dried
100ml olive oil
6 free-range eggs, hard-boiled, peeled and cut into quarters lengthways
1 teaspoon Dijon mustard
Juice of 1 lemon
Celery salt
Small bunch of flat-leaf parsley, leaves stripped
1 large teaspoon capers or caperberries
1 teaspoon chopped anchovies
Freshly ground black pepper

Lightly dress the cress with a small drizzle of olive oil. Place the quartered eggs on top of the cress.

Make a dressing with the Dijon mustard, lemon juice, olive oil and a small pinch of celery salt. Generously spoon the thick dressing over the eggs and cress.

Roughly chop the parsley and capers or caperberries, mix with the anchovies, add a pinch of pepper and just enough olive oil to make the mixture runny and finally pour this over the top of the salad so that the two dressings mingle.

The Perfect Fried Egg!

Luca D'Alfonso of The Fumbally Café in Dublin taught us to make The perfect fried egg – so simple, and always commented on, people notice there is something really extra, it is the textures of course?

1 fresh free-range egg
4 tablespoons olive oil
Freshly ground black pepper

Separate the yolk from the white while the 4 tablespoons (you do need this much) of oil are heating to shimmer in a small frying pan. Add the white, which will boil up and form a crisp edge with large air bubbles. After about 30 seconds of the white cooking, gently lower the golden yolk onto the centre of the white and spoon the boiling oil over the yolk until it goes opaque on the surface. Serve it hot on great bread with the oil poured aroundc– lots of pepper if you are using a duck egg!

Avgolémono

I can't imagine our house without this soup – as stock from the chicken bones is a weekly event in one or other of our kitchens, Avgolémono will be somewhere around Gubbeen most weeks. I reckon we've all got our little twists on how to improve it, but basically it comes down to amalgamating the egg yolks and lemons into a great chicken stock.

SERVES 3–4

- 1 tablespoon olive oil
- 1 carrot, finely chopped
- 1 celery stick, finely chopped
- 1 onion, finely chopped
- Small bunch of parsley, stalks and leaves chopped separately
- 1.5 litres chicken, duck or goose stock
- 2 bay leaves
- Sprig of thyme
- 4 tablespoons Basmati rice
- 4 free-range egg yolks
- Juice of 2 lemons
- Salt and freshly ground black pepper

Put the olive oil, carrot, celery, onion and chopped parsley stalks in a large soup pot and fry over a low heat until the vegetables have softened. Season generously and add the stock, bay leaves and thyme. Bring to the boil and simmer gently with a lid on for about 30 minutes until the vegetables are cooked and their goodness is realeased into the stock.

In a separate pan, boil the rice separately in a pan of salted water for about 15 minutes until just cooked but still with a little bite, then drain.

Strain the soup broth through a sieve and discard the chopped vegetables. Do not return the broth to the boil; allow it to cool down slightly.

Whisk the egg yolks and lemon juice together in a bowl, then pour into the broth and mix in well. This will turn the soup a lovely pale yellow and slightly thicken it as the yolks heat. Don't boil it or you will get scrambled eggs!

Check the seasoning. Serve in bowls with a generous amount of the cooked rice at the bottom and sprinkled with chopped parsley leaves.

SERVES 2–3

- 1 litre chicken stock
- 2 tablespoons Basmati rice or orzo pasta
- Salt and freshly ground black pepper
- 4 free-range egg yolks
- Juice of 1½ lemons

VARIATION

This version of Avgolémono makes a quick warming and filling lunch if you are in a hurry.

Bring the chicken stock to the boil and add the rice or orzo pasta. Boil for about 15 minutes until the rice or pasta is just cooked, and season well.

Whisk the egg yolks and lemon juice together. Whisk a ladleful of the hot broth into the eggs, then, off the heat, whisk the lemon mixture into the chicken stock, little by little.

The Great Boiled Chicken with Spanish Rice

We mostly rear poultry for eggs, and we have lots of pure breeds. Occasionally we have reared birds for the table but have never bonded that well with the rather fat, lazy breeds that we can source locally. If we could find Poulet de Bresse, I think we might do more. We are blessed, though, to have always known people who rear table fowl with great care and understand the process. Mostly this involves investing in what the birds eat from the time they hatch, plus of course ensuring that they can exercise, peck and scratch for food and interact with each other in an environment that is clean and gives them enough room, preferably outside. Those are the requirements for lovely strong healthy birds with deep-flavoured meat.

SERVES UP TO 8

For the chicken

1 tablespoon sunflower oil
2 onions, sliced
5 garlic cloves, crushed
2 carrots, roughly chopped
1 large leek, chopped
1 celery stick, chopped
Small bunch of flat-leaf parsley, stalks and leaves chopped separately
5 sprigs of thyme
3 bay leaves
1 litre chicken stock, if you have some
1 whole, happy chicken, about 1.5kg
750ml dry white wine – marsala or sherry would also work but use only 200–250ml
Salt and freshly ground black pepper

Select a pot large enough to accommodate your bird submerged in liquid along with all the veg and herbs. Place it over the heat, add the oil and gently fry the onions, garlic, carrots, leek and celery with a pinch of salt until they colour lightly. Add the herbs (reserving some of the chopped parsley leaves for the garnish) and the stock (if using). Now add the bird and the white wine. Top the liquid up with water and bring gently to the boil. Season with salt and black pepper to taste, making the stock as salty as you want the bird to taste. Gently simmer for 1 hour or up to 1½ hours if your bird is a little bigger. When it is cooked, remove from the heat and allow to sit in the pot, covered with a lid.

Time to cook the rice. A heavy pan with a lid, such as a Le Creuset, makes life so much easier and gives a superior result when cooking rice. Melt the butter over a medium heat and fry the onions with the thyme. When the onions are browned, add the rice and stir to coat in the fat.

Stirring constantly, ladle in enough poaching liquor from the boiled chicken to cover the rice by 2cm. Bring to the boil, then cook over a low heat with the lid on for 15 minutes. Turn off the heat and remove the lid. Fork the cooked rice to release some of the steam, remove and discard the thyme and pop the lid back on.

For the rice
25g butter
2 onions, diced
3 sprigs of thyme
500g Basmati rice
250g cooking chorizo, chopped small
1 red pepper, deseeded and diced
1 fennel bulb, thinly sliced widthways
2 tablespoons pine kernels
Finely grated zest of 1 unwaxed lemon
Olive oil

Retrieve your chicken from the pot, pick the meat from the carcass and keep warm. Keep the carcass for a future stock.

Fry the chorizo, red pepper and fennel in a large, hot pan – the fat in the chorizo will leach out, giving you ample for frying. When the fennel is golden, add the pine kernels followed by the cooked rice. It should all be a wonderful amber colour. Lastly mix in the lemon zest.

Spoon the rice into the middle of a deep dish and place the picked chicken over the top. Finish with an additional ladle of stock, a drizzle of olive oil and the reserved chopped parsley leaves.

This would be wonderful with Clovisse's Fresh Garden Salad (see page 206).

Roast Crown of Goose

Goose will always be a celebration dish – the bird itself is large and its meat is very rich, so it lends itself to feeding a big table full of family. The reason for removing the legs is that they always overcook and dry out; here you have the perfectly roasted breast and you can use the legs to make a delicious confit another day. Use the stuffing on page 79.

SERVES **5–6**

EQUIPMENT
Digital temperature probe

1 crown of goose (about 4kg)
Salt

Preheat the oven to 110°C/gas mark ¼.

Prick the goose skin all over with a needle. Sprinkle salt over the skin and rub it in. Place the goose, skin-side down, in a large frying pan or roasting tray and start to render the fat by cooking over a low to medium heat. The goose will start to cook in its own fat, but if the heat is too high this won't happen and the skin will burn. You're looking for an even golden colour all over, so do move the bird around the pan to achieve this.

Place the browned crown on a rack in a roasting tin and transfer to the oven. Roast for up to 2 hours before probing with the thermometer. How long the goose will take to cook depends on the performance of each individual oven, the weight of your bird and what temperature the crown is when it goes into the oven – a digital temperature probe is essential for this method. Probe the breast at its fattest point, stopping when you think you've reached the middle spot between the bone and the skin. If you estimate the breast is 4cm at its fattest aim to take the reading from a depth of 2cm. If the probe reads 55–56°C, it's ready. At this point remove the bird from the oven, cover and allow to rest for at least 15 minutes before carving.

Serve with Brussels sprouts and Proper Roast Potatoes (see page 221).

Goose Liver Pâté

This was the first thing Fingal cooked as a boy. If we ever have our own livers from the fowl here, this is exactly how we still make a little liver pâté. If you do have your own duck, chicken or goose to slaughter, be extra careful not to get any of the bile onto the liver: it is in a little green sac next to the liver and is brutally bitter. Trim off any sinews too, as they will not sieve or process – the texture of the liver must be silky.

SERVES 4

Goose or other poultry livers of your choice, approximately 150g
Equal weight of butter to liver
1–2 garlic cloves, finely chopped
1 shallot, diced
1 tablespoon Brandy
1 sprig of thyme
1 sage leaf
Grated zest of ½ lemon
Salt and freshly ground black pepper

Check the livers carefully for any sinews and remove them. Warm half the butter in a heavy-bottomed pan. Add the garlic and shallot and cook until softened. Add the livers and carefully brown them on both sides – don't overcook them; they really should be pink in the middle. As they heat add the brandy, herbs and salt and pepper.

Tip the contents of the pan into a food processor or blender and process this mixture until smooth. If it seems too lumpy, add more soft butter.

Transfer to a small pot, leaving room to seal the top, then chill. The pâté must be well chilled before you pour the clarified butter over it.

Meanwhile, melt the remaining butter in a pyrex bowl or measuring jug in a moderate oven until it is fully melted, then let the molten butter stand until it separates leaving the golden yellow clarified butter on top and the milky section below. Pour the butter gently on top of the pâté. Then sprinkle with the lemon zest. This tastes even better after a night in the fridge.

The pâté should keep for up to a week in the fridge if sealed well with the clarified butter.

Goose Stuffing

This is a traditional West Cork stuffing for the Christmas goose. It really complements goose as the potatoes soak up some of the wonderful fat from this rich bird. It is simple and, like many great simple dishes, it is authentic. The sage and thyme travel through the potatoes and lift the whole roast to another level.

SERVES 8

- 450g floury potatoes, cut into even-sized pieces
- 1 tablespoon olive oil
- 2 onions, chopped
- Large bunch of fresh sage
- 6–8 sprigs of fresh thyme
- Salt and freshly ground black pepper

Par-boil the potatoes for 10 minutes, then drain.

Meanwhile, heat the olive oil in a large pan and sauté the onions until transparent, not browned. Chop some of the sage leaves and add to the pan (keep the rest of bunch as it goes into the cavity). Season the goose cavity.

Chop the potatoes, which should still be firm, until semi-mashed, and mix in the onions and chopped sage. Season well. Push the remainder of the bunch of sage and the thyme to the back of the goose cavity. Put in the potato stuffing, leaving a good amount of air space at the top of the cavity, which acts like an oven, while the stuffing is a sort of sponge for the goose juices and some of its lovely fat too.

3

THE DAIRY

A CHEESE production day begins early. Tom will have started milking at 6 in the morning. He is first in to the dairy to turn on the heater for the mould-washing machine and to start up the boiler for our pasteuriser. The first milk will hit the big wooden vat by 7am. It comes in through a long white 'sock' filter to catch stray cow hairs or any dust off the udders.

Our cheeses, like all marketed foods, are licensed, and these licences are issued under EU law. Regulation extends all the way to our herd, which is tested for its general health and specifically the absence of TB and other illnesses that could be passed on to humans. Even the land itself is inspected to check that our farming practices meet legal requirements: for example, how much slurry we spread on it and the number of grazing animals per acre. The water used in the food-production rooms, along with each and every aspect of the production, are all covered by the EU legal agreement we enter into in order to be licensed for putting our cheeses into the marketplace. So it is quite a paper trail we work to each morning, from blackboards up in the milking parlour with messages from Tom to John our milker on individual animals' health or calving dates, to notes on the exact temperature of the morning milk. We have come a very long way from the romance of an old milk cow and a pike of hay.

Each morning, for the dairy to start production, John and Tom have to pass the freshly drawn milk through a refrigerated bulk tank to bring the milk down to the regulation under 5°C. It is then immediately piped into the dairy through a lined hole in the wall (in a previous life this liner was an old stainless-steel milk caddy, its perfectly fitting cap the lid). From here, the milk is filtered again carefully and the temperature games begin, from 5°C up to 75°C for 15 seconds, then down to 29°C in the holding tube and then through into the vat. Rose or Tom has to be alert from the moment milk first starts to flow; the morning starts with this quite concentrated test – cheesemakers always have a thermometer in their hand. This is then the end of the morning's hectic roller-coaster regulatory period for the milk. From this point on, the kinder, productive process of cheesemaking can begin.

The two vats at Gubbeen are Dutch-made. They are stainless steel with wooden-slatted sides. After years of scrubbing the wood has taken on a rather good, bleached look and the steel inside is polished to a shine. By 7.30am both vats will be filling, and the room is awake with warmth and good milk scents.

At 8 o'clock everyone is hands on: Rose, Monica, Eileen, Diane, Françoise, Maggie, Siobhan and Brian all working to take out yesterday's batch of cheeses from the moulds and move them into the brine baths, then set up the moulds for washing in the big grumbling industrial washer. We love this machine. It was our first big investment – before we bought it our mornings used to be taken up by four women

working for 2 hours, or two women working for 4 hours, scrubbing the moulds by hand, all done to a sterile finish, not just the usual wash down. Now this shining example of good engineering bangs the moulds into shape in half the time, and with a finish that you can see your face in. It has liberated us from the laborious scrubbing that used to dominate the morning, and the time can now be used to much better effect, working on the quality details.

When all of this activity is in full swing there is a huge timpani of noise, the stainless-steel moulds banging to release the cheeses, the steel cages of moulds being rolled up the ramp into the washer, air compressors hissing, washer, hoses, taps and the morning chat at full volume – then suddenly, silence!

Once the milk has filled the vats and the lactic starter cultures have been added to provide the acidity for the rennet to work with, there is a crucial silent step. Rennet is a catalyst and its subtle meshing of the proteins is really helped if the room is calm and vibration-free, so we pay this natural process the respect of silence. For 20–30 minutes the room empties, apart from Rose our cheesemaker who likes to test temperature and pH quietly at this time.

There is really dynamic biology going on in the vat now, the developing lactobacilli starter cultures in the warm milk guzzling on the lactose milk sugars and multiplying at a great rate, the enzymes in the rennet interacting with this acidity and meshing the protein. The cheesemakers have to monitor the heat and the development of the acidity at this time really carefully as this is where the unique quality of our cheese is controlled: one degree more or less of pH value and it will not be Gubbeen, one degree lost in the temperature and we would be chasing the vat for the rest of the morning, trying to catch the right texture.

Cheesemaking is a three-dimensional process in that we will be making cheese for tomorrow's brine today, and today's brine will be emptied of yesterday's make which will be moved to the curing rooms. There is a great bond between everyone as we work together in and around these processes. We all have to support each other; if the curing is slow we all cure, or if unexpectedly there is a new order and cheeses have to be packed and weighed for a waiting lorry, we all pile in there, and of course there is cleaning, never ending, checking, cleaning and hygiene.

So, by around 11 o'clock the first vat is now set, all the temperatures and pH tests showing it is the right moment for the cut to begin. The long multi-bladed cutters are fitted to the arm of the vat and, very slowly at first, the firm curd is opened up.

It's a long process, the separating of curd and whey. As the blades begin to open up the set milk, the pale green whey starts to seep out. Cheesemakers work with the warmth of the vat, the acidity and the buffeting of the little curds against one another to shrink them, forming curds by squeezing out the whey. The tools here are our hands and the blades gently and consistently stirring and separating the curds as they form, drawing out the whey from the solid proteins that will become the cheese.

At the same time, down the ramp from the production area, yesterday's newly salted cheeses are brought from the brine baths into the first curing room. There they sit and rest for a day in the warmth and humidity while the

chemical changes of the production settle and the salts and acidity are balanced out with the proteins, enzymes and fats of the very white, very firm brined cheeses.

This is day one of the cure.

In our curing rooms Diane and Siobhan carry out the ancient work of curing. I prefer the French term *affinage*, meaning refining, as our word 'curing' implies there is something wrong, whereas it is far more about bringing out and refining the product. In any case, it is the skills of watching and understanding how the rinds are reacting to the salts and the newly inoculated little seeds of the Gubbeen rind flora that has been introduced on day two by Siobhan and Diane who wash each cheese by hand to inoculate or seed the rinds with our own unique combination of flora, including *Microbacterium gubbeenense*.

Of course, if the production is not finely judged and the moulding not exactly timed, if the cutting has been rushed, or the temperatures have jumped or plunged – all of which can happen for many reasons – the cheeses that are brined and transferred to the curing rooms will not look untoward for about four days, but then awful things can happen! Soft rinds can split, the cheese under the rind can start to run, the yeasts on the rind can proliferate and the rind itself can become rank and sticky... on and on the list of cheese problems can build, and they are not for the faint-hearted: mouldy, sticky, running, bloated cheeses with hard hearts instead of the soft pink, bloomy, bouncy and healthy little Gubbeens we love and work towards.

Yes, cheese curing is a skill.

Affinage is a science that you can perfect as a food technology degree, but for us it is with the shared knowledge that Diane and I have built up and acquired – over 16 years for Diane, and in my case 38 years – that we manage to talk and sniff our way through the morning's worries most days with solutions that range from fine-tuning the temperature or humidity levels to adding more salt, or some wine, or sometimes vinegar to adjust the acidity. In extreme cases the cheeses can get pushed out into a spot we know as the Frog Hole, which is in fact a damp, airless back hall, the oldest part of the dairy, that usually has some hexing effect on even the most grim rinds.

Back in the production rooms, while curing is underway below, in the vats the cut is speeding up a little. The pH and temperature are the only measurements that give Rose any solid indication of what is going on in this white, and by now pale green, world of curds and whey. That, and Rose's years of experience, her nose, her sense of touch and monkey-cunning that are key to a good cheesemaker.

The cut curds will be shrinking slowly and, we hope, uniformly under the pressure of heat as it slowly mounts, along with *frottage* – the bumping and rubbing of the little curds against each other – and then osmosis too as the acidity builds in the vat and more whey is drawn out. Rose's skill now is all about keeping this huge (2,000-litre) vat all as one – as far as is possible: no little lumps of unstirred curds, no hot spots or sunken cool bits lurking at the bottom. Uniformity is really important; this stage is back-aching hard work.

When Tom is cheesemaker, having more strength in his shoulders, he will use the mechanics of the vat quite differently from Rose. We all have our methods: I always brought the vats in far more slowly than either Tom or Rose, never using the clock as a guide. For me it was all about the curd, whereas Rose always has one eye on time yet all three of us make Gubbeen that is within an inch of being the same end product.

I am confident just to believe that there is some invisible discipline at work and the chain of personalities involved is somehow a part of the cheese itself.

By around 12.30pm, the vat 'comes in' – that is, the curd is ready to be moulded, with the moisture mostly worked out. It is the tension of the curd that is so important, involving lots of hard work and continuous stirring to open up the masses that naturally build up. Although the arm of the vat is working with you, as the cutters can be turned back to front to become stirring bars, on the whole it is the strong arms of the cheesemaker that get this job done.

The tables, that in the morning were covered with cheese from yesterday's make, now carry the clean stainless-steel moulds, sterilised like the tables themselves and ready to be filled. The still-hot moulds, just out of the washer, are set into a Lego-like design of 300 large ones and 250 small ones with 8 extra-large white and often 6 tiny heart-shaped moulds for Clovisse's wedding 'cheese cakes'.

Everything is ready for the big event, the 'vatting' or moulding, all done as fast as possible to achieve the uniformity that is so important. The whole room fills up again with all hands and Rose, like the starter at a horse race, waits for the pH (or is it the squeak on the teeth?), as she tests the curd then 'they're off'. It's part choreography, part sport, as everyone trawls curds from the vat into the base of the perforated moulds and hits the table with them, lid on, just as the second pair of hands puts the next mould down, while at the bottom of the table Diane will be turning them, lid off, then she twitches the formed curd out and flips it, lid back on. After the first turn, kilo weights are put on the lid to ensure that an even pressure takes the shaped lid down as the curds are losing weight at a great rate now, shrinking down in the mould as the whey pours out.

The room is warm – in summer, very warm – essential, as although the solids are now magicked out of the liquid state they started in, there is no stopping yet for the lactobacilli which are still working away, building the pH curve that is vital for the finished cheese.

By lunchtime all the tables are full, the vats are empty and the moulds have been turned twice. The cheese is made and is draining. For a while the dairy is quiet again. Lunch!

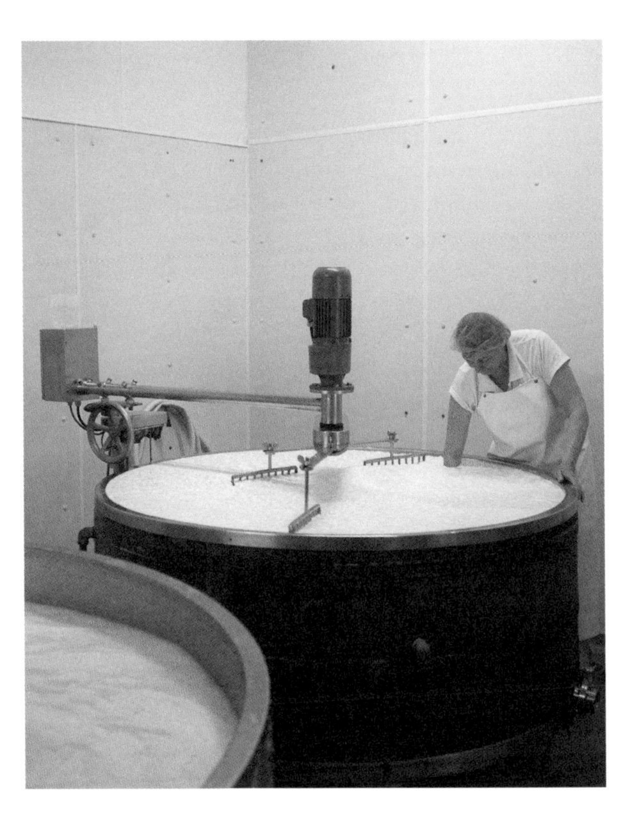

Microbacterium Gubbeenense

The unique flavour of Gubbeen and the story of how we came to have a bacterium named after our little farm dairy in West Cork is where pure science, as organised scepticism, meets tradition.

It is not so unlikely, this coming together of academic microbiology and a handmade cheese, when it is understood as a study of biodiversity. At the very end of the 90s, a time when the new farmhouse cheese industry in Ireland was still in its infancy, a rather tangled relationship had developed between regulatory bodies and our movement. We were actively growing the business in the early 80s and beginning to earn some following as the first pioneers – ourselves, Milleens, Coolea, Boile, Durrus, Gigginstown – won awards both here and in the UK, where we were finding like-minded markets.

The UK was taking a stand for the conservation of its ancient territorial cheeses, which were under threat at the time, and making a determined effort to protect their old dairying traditions. It proved to be a fertile market for Irish cheeses and, although in many respects our food culture was flourishing, food was mostly imported, cheese was Cheddar, and meat production was being guided down the industrial route.

The stage was wide open for a bunch of people who were prepared to try to introduce new ideas in dairying and farming methods, in part drawn from Europe and yet very connected to early Irish milk production.

So when Milleens, Durrus and Gubbeen first arrived in London we were met with enthusiasm. Here were new soft and semi-soft cheeses, handmade in West Cork, made in small quantities and where we all farmed seaonally and in a climate that lent itself to very high-quality milk. These cheeses really spoke, and smelt, of traditional systems of production. Within ten years, though, we had arrived at a crossroads. If we wanted a chance to market abroad, regulatory compliance spelled out one clear message: pasteurise.

I think it was during this time that the work we had done at Gubbeen in making consistency our goal came to our aid. We had a good and fairly consistent rind. For me, it offered some sort of solution to the pasteurisation problem we were facing: pasteurise the milk, then work to develop the rind to allow the unique qualities of the cheese to shine through.

From the earliest days of the farmhouse cheese dairies we had found support in University College, Cork. They ran courses in microbiology, they allowed us access to their libraries and lecturers, and it was here that Tom and I met Professor Pat Fox from the Department of Food Science and Technology, and Doctor Tim Cogan from Dairy Product Research in Teagasc in Fermoy. They had a young star PhD student, Noelle Brennan, who was doing her doctorate in the very subject that, in part, could best supply the knowledge I badly needed. Noelle's dissertation, published in 2000, studied the relationship between the various natural flora growths from our farm, and which ones flourished on our rinds, and demonstrated that there was significant proof that certain strains (which she identified and named) supported each other and by proliferating can reduce the risk of pathogen contamination.

We now work each day with those cultures that Noelle's study identified from our rinds, *Microbacterium gubbeenense* being one of them. Not surprisingly, it thrives in our curing rooms and, along with two other microbacteria that were also isolated as being dominant natural local strains, it is responsible for the strength and recognisable character of our rinds. Before Noelle's work, we had been importing at great expense cultures that were commercially available to support rind development. This study showed that within about ten days the traditional local ones had driven them back and were dominant.

We are hugely grateful for this work and happy to have the Gubbeen name attached to such a relevant piece of research in the cheese world.

Brining

When the cheeses – still as white as milk – freed from their moulds, hit the brines, they are in transformation. More than simply a salt-and-water brine solution that protects the cheeses from contamination, three processes immediately affect them, the salts slow down the acid production as it is drawn into the cheeses, the rinds start to toughen as the highly saline brines draw whey out and also some of the local flora present in these brines will become embedded on the rinds and start to influence the next stage of curing room work.

To keep this crucial stage under some sort of control takes a lot of perseverance. We check the brine daily, adjusting it accordingly as the seasons and throughput of cheeses dip and raise the chemical balance of the brine.

We have nursed our brines along for nearly 20 years now. To ensure they keep well, we sieve the brines daily to remove the tiny bits of cheese that fall in, continuously monitor the salt, pH and temperature levels, and we also test the bacteria content to be sure the brines are clean. Then, once a month, we syphon off from the bottom a portion of the brine and replace it with fresh water, and the monitoring starts all over again.

Brining brings more, much more, than just the salt to the newly formed crust or rind. It is a vital step and it needs to be supported as a complex ingredient of Gubbeen as well as a hygiene measure for the maturing cheeses. Once the cheeses have spent their allocated time in brine – giving them a 1.8–2 per cent salt content – they are moved down to the curing rooms for the next stage in the process which introduces its own, very dynamic component, almost a form of microbiological gardening.

Curing the rind

As the door between the production area and the first curing room closes, there is a pronounced change. After the steel and noise of the production room the atmosphere in the curing rooms is rather like a cave, warm and damp, and in here the scent of the fresh cheeses is sweet and buttery. This first room is low-ceilinged and small-windowed with a wet stone floor and very high humidity. The cheeses are stacked on beautiful interlocking wire racks and are piled high along the back of the curing room walls to rest for the first day of curing.

For the next ten days the cheeses in our three curing rooms will be undergoing an almost complete transformation as the rinds develop their unique growth of the Gubbeen flora while the body of the cheese metabolises the proteins and the enzymes and lactic bacteria work through the fats and casein (milk protein).

By the second day our rested cheeses are ready to be inoculated – or seeded – with the *gubbeenense* wash. This we dilute with clean water until it looks like pale tea and then smear it, using our hands, onto each cheese for four days, rubbing the whole cheese with the solution and turning it each day.

By the fourth day there is a clear change in the rind, it is softening, the yeasts are beginning to work into the surface of the young cheese and take root, by day five it develops a light bloom, like the bloom on grapes picked straight from vines that carry their own local yeast.

By the fifth day we are changing our wash to salt and water. No more inoculation is needed; the daily rubbing and turning of the cheese has spread the spores that have formed and the *gubbeenense* flora is multiplying and taking a strong hold. The salt creates a very safe environment and the salt-loving *gubbeenense* is starting to grow strongly. Pinkish-brown colonies are showing all over the rinds and will be encouraged by the daily turning and washing that bruises the tiny spores open and encourages more seeds to spread and root.

By the end of the seventh or eighth day we often use a wine wash to encourage a balance between all the various micro-organisms. Wine, like salt, supports a clean pathogen-free rind, while its natural acidity is compatible with our flora. Throughout the age-old history of cheesemaking, this partnership of cheeses, salt and wine has been used happily.

If we see unwanted moulds forming, the trick is to lower the pH fast, and a stronger acidic ally is brought in – vinegar. We use organic cider vinegar, diluted according to need: strong for the blue moulds (*penicillium*) and weak for the *mucor* or cat's-hair moulds.

The final migrant to the rind is the lovely soft white bloom of the *Penicillium camemberti*, which is a form of mould we do want. This grows once the yeast and the *gubbeenense* have settled into a good undercoat and are working strongly. When this final white bloom develops and the three flourish together, they deepen the flavours, bringing the mushroom scents and lovely boggy notes to the rind as their mycelium roots work down through the paste and metabolise the proteins, giving a softening and bounce to the body of the cheese within.

After fourteen days the cheese is ready to enter a cooler life cycle. It can now be either packed or cured on.

We pack our ripe cheeses in waxed paper to maintain a nice little microclimate between the rind and the paper while it endures the chill chain of transport to markets all over the world. Transportation temperature is a constant worry for us as, sadly, regulations require it to be under 5°C, which is far too cold for a truly happy rind growth. Good cheesemongers have to work with a combination of regulation and cheese savvy, which is not always the same thing!

Once the cheeses are ripe enough to pack, we can choose a few to keep on and cure for longer here at the dairy in our own curing-room conditions which are ideal for the ageing. These are our vintage Gubbeens. In the last few years we have been ageing the smoked cheeses for up to six months and more. This black waxed cheese offers a lot of potential for making an 'aged' cheese that is completely different from the semi-soft, original smoked version. As it ages it loses moisture and becomes a harder and very intensely flavoured original all of its own.

All our cheeses undergo the same packaging process, and there is a vast amount of food regulation to observe in terms of labelling with weights and measures and the new key to tracking all food: traceability. This involves each and every cheese being identified by its production date, which relates back to all the notes we keep each day on the make. In an average audit we would have to track a cheese from the point the cow was milked, all the way through the curing, to the point when the cheese was dispatched to its customer. So the batch numbers follow the cheese all the way to our customers. So the paper trails are pretty complex and a lot of time at Gubbeen is spent on lists, computers, dispatch notes and head scratching.

I sometimes think, as the cheeses leave Gubbeen Dairy, that they are bit like children going off to a party – you wash them and dress them up to look their very best, then hope they will behave themselves while they are away on their own! All the care and attention they get we hope comes through to our customers, bringing them the delicate rinds and very distinctive flavours we've worked to create.

GUBBEEN CHEESE
washed cheese made and cured
from the milk of the Gubbeen Herd.
Gubbeen Cheese Ltd., Gubbeen House
Schull, Co Cork, Ireland
Telephone +353 (0)28 28231 cheese@gubbeen.com
Fax: +353 (0)28 28609 www.gubbeen.com

Notes on Milk

Given that milk is the key ingredient for any home dairy production – yogurt, butter or simple cheese – I hope it might be useful to share a few ideas with you here about the subject of milk quality.

Milk is complex and raw milk is very complex and very vulnerable. The quality of milk doesn't start with the bucket, bottle or carton it comes in; it begins with the animal and the land where it is produced.

There is a lot of ongoing debate about the health of animals that produce milk for human consumption and more and more tests are suggested for dairy suppliers to be sure that these foods are free from any disease risk that can be transferred from animal to man. The pasteurisation debate still goes on, and the balance between nutrition and food safety remains a concern for all cheesemakers. It is not simply a question of all milk being good for you. The one basic rule is that it's never what you can see in dairying that you should be concerned about, but what you can't see. Bacterial contamination is very common, so you want to buy your milk only from trained and dedicated milkers. The milking process is not straightforward and I respect so much the men and women who, morning and evening, season after season, will their herds into action and their machines to function perfectly to put milk on our tables.

Milking is one of the oldest agricultural traditions we have, and fresh raw milk from healthy cows, sheep or goats is one of the greatest foods on earth. It is still the primary source of nutrition for infants worldwide and at its best is a wonderful thing. Sadly, it is potentially not always safe. The last thing I would ever want to do is put people off making delicious dairy products, so I feel it is worth gaining just a little knowledge before you start.

These days, buying milk from commercial outlets in urban centres means it will be pasteurised; it may also have been processed to standardise the amount of protein or butter fat it contains, or it could even be Ultra Heat Treated (UHT), which makes it 'ultra safe'. Ironically, perhaps, none of these milks are the best raw material for homemade dairy produce. They taste slightly of caramel and they have certainly lost some of their vitamins and enzymes. I am sure that anyone interested in making their own yogurt or cheese is considering the nutrition of their family, so this means searching out a really experienced farmer who understands the milking and animal husbandry required to produce super-safe raw milk. Happily, there are many of these very valuable and respected farmers. So if near you there is a farm or small holding where there is already a tradition of milk processing, you are in safe hands. I would suggest asking at farmers' markets or good cheesemongers who are in touch with their suppliers and have an understanding of what 'quality' milk really means. The added bonus here is that the more people ask for quality raw milk, the more accessible the supply will become.

Really good milk is under 24 hours old, it will have been chilled to lower than 5°C and the animals it comes from will have been screened for several of the contagious conditions that sadly can be present in herds and flocks. The milk will also have been bacterially tested either at source or by the seller on several occasions and this will give them, and you, confidence in their milk for your dairy projects.

I know all this sounds rather clinical, and I have at times been critical myself of some of the demands that regulation makes on dairy farmers, but it stands as a protection for consumers, and no one can really argue with that. Once you have sourced quality fresh milk, all you need to think about is always to keep it chilled and stored in clean containers, then *really enjoy* the satisfying process of making your own yogurt, butter and cheeses for your family!

Basic Recipe For a Home-Made Farm Cheese

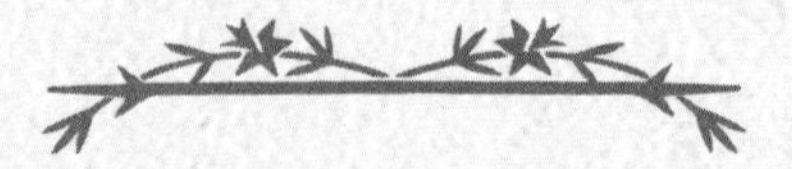

One of the nicest things a novice cheesemaker can do during the warm sunny days of summer, when cattle are grazing on sweet sun-enriched grass, is to find a good source for milk and plan your Christmas cheese. A cheese made between June and August will have plenty of time to cure on for the most wonderful Christmas present to your family.

As this is for a good long cure, be brave and make a big cheese. Small 500g cheeses will cure fast as lovely young lactic-flavoured experiments (a good place to start with cheesemaking perhaps?) but for Christmas cheeses for a family table you need something with presence, so invest in at least 10 litres of milk – 20 litres would be even better. Please remember that the final curd you will be pressing into a mould as solids will be only a fraction of the liquids in volume. I am using the ratio of 10 litres of milk for *approximately* 1kg of cheese. I use the word approximately with real feeling as cheesemaking is rather like handwriting: we all lend our own slant to the end product and this recipe is to guide and encourage, the final result will have as much of your interpretation as it has of my guidelines.

EQUIPMENT

Milton for sterilisation This contains chlorus, which kills bacteria on contact so it does a thorough job of cleaning your equipment. *But* cheesemaking is all about growing bacteria in the form of lactobacilli, so you must rinse and dry off the equipment carefully! Steep everything in a sinkful of cold water with the right amount of Milton for at least 10 minutes. Rinse, then leave to drain-dry on a clean surface – all traces of the chlorus will dissipate.

20-litre stock pot or 10-litre stainless-steel mixing bowl

Dairy thermometer Do find a good thermometer that is accurate or buy two cheap ones and use them both and take an average reading.

A Mould for the cheese curd If borrowing a 2kg cheese mould from a friendly neighbouring dairy is not an option, then vandalise a nice brand-new plastic bucket! Choose food-grade plastic and sterilise it well. For 20 litres of milk you will need to press down curds that will finally weigh about 2–2.5kg and be about 8–10cm high. The top of the mould should be about 25cm diameter. I see these small pails in good hardware shops. They should be made from plastic thin enough to enable you to bore holes all around the base and up the sides (say 1 hole every 2cm) for draining the whey. Make the holes bigger than pin holes but not so big that they are going to leave impressions on the final cheese. If you are using 10 litres of milk choose a smaller container – your final cheese will be over 1kg so you want your bucket or pail to be about 18cm diameter.

Length of cheesecloth muslin You can improvise with fine net curtain, linen or loosely woven cotton, but avoid manmade fibres as you will need to sterilise this by either boiling or by soaking it in Milton.
Large stainless steel spoon One with holes in perhaps
Long-bladed stainless-steel knife
Plastic or stainless-steel colander
Sterilising agent

A note on heating Slow, gentle heat to prevent burning the milk is best done in a bain-marie system with a saucepan of gently simmering water under your stainless-steel bowl with the milk in it.

If you are using the big stock pot, do keep the milk stirred well.

INGREDIENTS

10–20 litres fresh, *quality* raw milk
Starter cultures Dried commercial starters or DVS (Direct Vat Starter) if you are near a cheesemaker who can let you have some, or 'live' yogurt, easy and often very good
Rennet Be aware that all rennet is different in strength! Be sure to read the instructions carefully. Rennet comes in different forms, liquid and pill, but in either form it contains enzymes that work on the fresh milk protein casein to give you a nice coagulation. If you get liquid rennet, do keep it in the fridge (not freezer) away from sunlight. We now use traditional or animal rennet extracted from the lining of the fourth stomach of the calf. Its active ingredients are the enzymes renin or chymosin, as well as pepsin. These should give you a perfect curd and, later in the curing period, your cheese will cure on developing good interesting flavours.
Dairy salt Any salt will do, but do buy pure salt with no additives that make it easy to pour or offer health benefits. Dairy salt has a nice rough honest quality and is designed to dilute and absorb.

METHOD

Day 1 – Acidification

If you know that the raw milk is the best quality and has been chilled immediately to under 5°C right after milking (do keep it cold during the trip back to your kitchen), you can go ahead with stage 1. Or, if you want to be sure the milk is just right, follow the heat-treating advice in the yogurt section (see page 112).

Pour the milk into an absolutely clean stainless-steel bowl or pot to heat to 29–30°C. (Leave a cupful aside in a clean jug for the renneting process which comes after this acidifying with starter being added.)

Add your starter culture. With dried cultures follow the supplier's instructions. The same applies to DVS – if it is still deeply frozen, do remember to give it longer to 'wake up' plus the acidification time, about 5 minutes more. If you are using live yogurt, add 1 teaspoon per litre of milk. Check your milk is at 30°C and maintain that temperature throughout – the milk with the starter added needs to acidify for 25 minutes.

Now take the reserved cupful of milk and add the correct amount of rennet (see the supplier's instructions).

Very gently stir the milk and rennet together and then add it slowly, using a circular action, to your milk at 30°C. Stir from the bottom of the pot to the top, for perhaps 30 seconds, then allow it to settle on its own. We actually empty the dairy at this stage and we don't have music playing, or people rushing by – whimsy, perhaps, but the principle is that this is a subtle and delicate stage when the enzymes in the rennet are meshing and trapping the solids of casein into the curds that in the next stage you will be cutting. This coagulation will take 20–30 minutes.

Coagulation Test

I think by now you will automatically be checking that your coagulation is at the right temperature – 30°C. Pressing very gently with your knuckle will show that there is a nice texture forming after 20 minutes. Take a knife and make a straight cut, not too deeply, 8–10cm long in the paste, then angle

the knife at a slant, insert it under the cut and slowly bring the knife up. The curd should snap open and the sides will be shiny and a little green whey will start to show in the incision. If the walls are soft and the curd does not snap open, wait another 5 minutes and repeat.

Cutting

By 'cutting' curd we are opening up as many sides as possible for the whey to leach out. So the idea is to make small dice about 2cm square. Your knife should be long enough to reach right to the bottom of the pot. Make the first cut gently and slowly north to south from one side to the other until the curd is all cut in strips, then cut gently and slowly from west to east in the same way.

Now angle the knife horizontally and slice across from the top to the bottom, again at the four different quarters; the result should be neat but not perfect little dice.

Don't get too caught up in the evenness of these dice, though, as the next part of the process is really dynamic. Whey will start to flow out from the curd which you have maintained at 30°C; if the temperature has dropped, you will need to gently start heating the pot again so the curds are floating in whey that is maintained at 30°C.

You don't want to shock the bacteria into slowing down their acid production at all and a lower temperature is exactly what would cause this.

The whey expulsion is all-important now and you have four actions working for you:

1. Osmosis (the passage of water from a weak to a strong solution).
2. *Frottage* (the bumping and rubbing of the curds against one another).
3. Heat will shrink the curds and expel whey.
4. The growing acidity will also shrink the curds and also expel whey.

I really recommend you use your hand for this: a good clean hand gives you so much more information and control than a spoon. (A lovely rule of thumb for well-washed hands is to rub and scrub them together using anti-bacterial soap for as long as it takes to sing 'Twinkle Twinkle Little Star'!)

Scalding

This is in fact heating gently, so turn on your heat source again – if you are using the bain-marie system. Organise the pot so that it is raised a little

higher over the water than before so the heating is slow. The starting point is 30°C and the end point will be 39°C.

This is an important constraint as you are probably using a mesophilic (moderate heat-loving) starter which will not thrive or even survive if you take it up too high – which means above 40°C. Given that you'll be expelling at least half of the whey from the curd at this stage using the four functions above, do take your time – at least 20–25 minutes.

Your hand is your best guide as you will be stirring from the bottom to the top of the pot, feeling for clumps of curd that are sticking together, searching out the big bits that you can slit with your thumbnail and generally managing the whole pot towards a uniform, gently heating, shrinking mass of similar-sized curds. Sounds easy? After 15 minutes, as the temperature reaches around 35°C, you will feel the tension building in the curds texture as they slowly become more and more like popcorn to look at, and start to feel denser and tighter.

At 25 minutes and at 39°C, if you are not satisfied that the curds are uniformly heated or sized, or if there are some curds that are still shiny and wet with whey inside them, keep going. One of the easiest ways to spoil the flavour of a cheese during ageing is to have trapped whey. There will still be bacteria present in these little shiny curds; they will be raising the acidity and you will get pockets with dry, acid flavours that are grainy and not bouncy. So take your time in the scalding and work it to a lovely uniformity.

Moulding

Keep the curds under the whey. Now prepare the mould by lining it with the muslin and set it on a draining board. Lift the curds into the mould as fast as is safe. (It might worry you how much there is, but remember how much the draining overnight will reduce this.) As soon as the curds are all piled into the mould, place the 'follower' on top (this is possibly the lid of the pail that you have cut to slip gently down on the top of the wrapped curd bundle). I would use a large jam jar full of water as a weight – it is clean and heavy.

After little more than 10 minutes, lift off the jam jar, then the follower, and pull out the muslin. Your curds will have magically formed into a mass, and now will be neither crumbling nor too fragile. At this point you can discard the muslin, turn the cheese carefully upside down and return it to the mould, then replace the follower and the jam jar.

In the first hour try to turn the cheese at least twice more. The shape will be thrilling as it shrinks pretty fast and the final cheese 'look' starts to appear.

Overnight the dynamics go on. The starter culture is still working for you, so do try to keep the cheese really pretty warm as it drains: a nice 20°C is perfect, if you can achieve it. At least don't let it chill or you will have a much harder job to do during the curing.

Now… a nice glass of wine and the smile of a job well done!

Day 2 – Curing (and Refining)

Early the next morning you need to take your cheese out of the mould. You will find that it has shrunk down a lot, it will have formed its final shape now, and it is not going to change in volume really from this point. The turning of the evening before should have given it a nice even look. You need to set up a rack on a draining board where you can manage the next two days of salting. This area needs to be clean and warm – the salt you are going to add will draw moisture out of the cheese and drip rather sticky whey around, so a bit of planning for isolating half your sink might be handy.

Sprinkle 2 heaped tablespoons of salt on the top of the cheese set on the rack and rub it well in and down along the sides – very important to remember the sides of the cheese need curing too. Leave the cheese to drip through the rack and absorb this salt for 24 hours.

Day 3

Turn your cheese over and repeat by adding 2 tablespoons of salt to the other side. Again, rub well in and down the sides. It will still be dripping a bit. Don't worry that you might be oversalting the sides – the salt travels right into the centre of your cheese via the little fat globules, and though it is applied to the sides twice some of this will of course run off as well as being drawn into the cheese body.

There are three functions salt performs: first, it is your primary curing defence against any contamination; second, it gives your cheese a nice, strong rind (as salt draws out moisture by osmosis, it creates a nicely toughened rind); and third, of course, it provides flavour. Cheese that doesn't have enough salt always seems to taste thin and lack depth.

Day 4

So, by day 4 you have effectively completed the 'curing' and from now you will only be maintaining and refining the rind. The amount of salt you have already introduced has done a great deal and you will simply top it up from now on with saline washes for another week.

The rind is still vulnerable but your cheese can be moved away from the sink now; it will have begun to dry and will no longer be losing moisture. I would keep it on the rack, though, as the rungs give the rind a nice pattern of lines and it also allows air to circulate over and under the cheese, which helps dry it. Find a resting place that is airy, not too humid and clean. Do protect your cheese from flies, as they can ruin all this work in one unguarded moment. Old pantries had lovely larders with fly screens (this is ideal); if you don't have one perhaps you can rig up a cake cloche or fly proofing with muslin, but be careful not to create an airless environment as this can encourage damaging moulds to attack your rinds at this early stage.

Cheese development and curing is a huge subject for which there are four-year degree courses, so I can only give you guidelines here. What I really advise now is to follow your instincts. If the cheese develops moulds, wash them off with a good salty solution; if it dries out and looks like cracking (hot summers are as troublesome as cold damp winter days), a good wet wash and rub will help. For the next ten days there should be a daily turn and wash with a saline solution (2 tablespoons of salt stirred into 1 litre of very clean water), or you can get creative with a white wine solution, or perhaps add some vinegar if you are finding the rinds a bit yeasty-smelling. Beer or a small glass of brandy added to the washing water will do something else: it will be cleaning and providing flavour, so keep washing, watching and experimenting.

As time passes the rind will respond uniquely to the conditions in your larder or back kitchen. How dry or damp, or warm or cold it is will affect your rind. Nearly all atmospheric conditions will be all right for the cheese as long as you have performed the original salting which will have strengthened the rind sufficiently to protect the body of the cheese inside.

A Note on Rind Washing

Rind washing is not a soaking process; it is done to moisten and clean the rind so that you need only enough salty water to rub evenly around the whole cheese, top, bottom and sides, smoothing and making it uniform – it should be 'greasy', not sopping or scoured. At ten days to two weeks old the cheese really should have a good rind. It should not be wet (unless you have just washed it), and if there is any rind growth it should not be long-haired moulds, but tight fine moulds that with each wash become a part of the rind in the way cement ages outside in the garden after a month of weathering.

Our Gubbeen develops a nice smooth yeasty rind by day 4 or 5, followed in the next week by a brownish-pink mushroomy-smelling growth

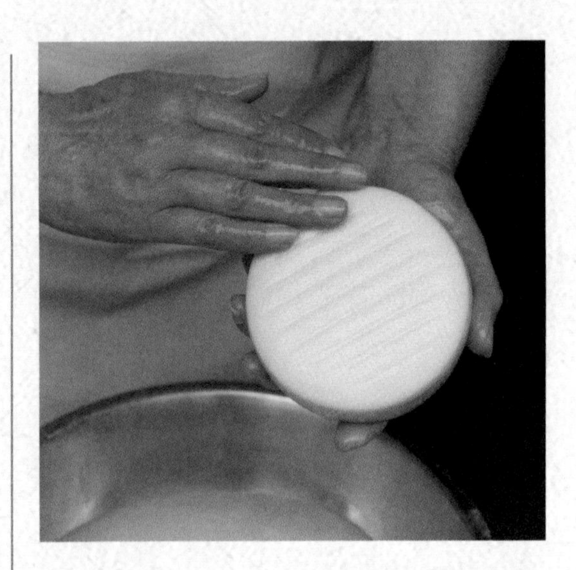

and then, as it ages, a white bloom overcoat. By three months this is a fairly thick and firm crust. Your cheese might have grey or blue-green patches; as long as they are washed into the rinds with salty water they will be fine and incorporate into a final crust.

People always ask me whether you can eat rinds, and I remember my mother chewing away at ancient Cheddars with rinds like linoleum. She said she loved the taste of the cellar; it's not for everyone, but in the right conditions I can see no reason why not. However, don't be pressured if you don't like it – give it to the dog!

Our smoked cheese is painted with a wax, which these days comes in a semi-liquid form – no more melting and dipping; we just paint it on to a perfectly dry, four-day-old brined rind and as it dries, it tightens. The wax is semi-permeable, allowing the cheese to breathe but protecting it and keeping the smoked flavours in.

You might find food wax easy to buy and certainly it is a very good solution and substitute to all that washing. Paint on two or three coats (allowing it to dry well between coats) and turn the cheese now and then as it ages.

So, a final thing to remember is to turn the cheese daily for at least ten days then, if you find you forget, or start to relax after this, that is fine! Whenever you think of it, flip the cheese over and watch as it develops. Ideally you want

to have made a cheese using the wonderful fresh milk that comes from cows grazing on pasture during August for the Christmas table – it will be a truly great present to your family!

Try to make more than one cheese so that you can taste them as they develop and get to know your preferred flavour. Do, though, try to hold off sampling for at least two weeks with the first one so there is some good acidity and a sense of real cheese.

By now you will know that cheesemaking involves very complex bits of chemistry and fermentation, but don't be daunted. The day will come when one of your cheeses will be just wonderful and you will relish this more than anything you have made before!

Development of Cheese Varieties

There are literally thousands of different cheeses in the world, which has led to the need to classify them according to various criteria. Of the general categories that are identified, the most commonly accepted is moisture content, which accounts for texture. This is further broken down by fat content and production methods, including curing or ripening, and finally by the curing systems: these are more an indicator of 'types'. Equally important is the source of the milk used – it can be from most lactating domestic animals: cows, goats, buffaloes, horses or sheep. Complex, yes, but this is a subject as influenced by geography, history and taste as wine production is. With wine, we are happy to learn about the grape, the region and the vintage, and so it is with cheeses.

Gubbeen cheese is classified as semi-soft, which puts it in the category of a moisture content of 40–50 per cent surface ripened, which refers to the curing method of washing the cheese to encourage its smear growth of rind flora, and it is made from cow's milk. The cheese is then classified as Irish, West Cork as the region. Good cheesemongers might add a detail like 'from a single farm herd', which is a clue to the size of our dairy and the farming system.

Which animal provides the milk will be the obvious distinguishing feature of the cheese – the white body of goat's or buffalo's cheese never alters, while cow's milk with its carotene content (particularly high in Ireland) will cause various shades of yellow (but don't be fooled by the Cheddars that have had an addition of annatto, a natural colouring derived from the seed of the achiote tree which also gives that strange dark orange to certain Territorial English cheeses like the Red Leicester).

Curing rooms are the unique places where the alchemy that transforms cheeses occurs. They arrive in these controlled areas as young salted curds and depart as white-bloomed Bries or blue Stiltons, or great hard Cheddars or Parmigiano-Regiano.

The relationship between our farm's milk and the cheese it makes is my favourite part of the cheesemaking process. The work that goes on in the curing rooms will keep me curious for the rest of my life, along with the developing research into the microbiology of these farm cheeses, where the signature character of a cheese is formed either on the rinds, or from the old wooden shelves of some of the more traditional dairies – shelves which are the source of some of the tiny influences on flavour, such as mites, spores or even microbes.

A cheese flavour develops not only from the chemistry that takes place in the body of the cheese, ageing and deepening the flavours, but is also hugely influenced by the curing environment, which brings out its full potential.

Week after week great truckles of Cheddar, bandaged to protect the rind, are slowly undergoing many biochemical processes supported by the temperature and humidity controls in these stores. Unlike Gubbeen, which is rind ripened with the growth of active flavour compounds on the rind (see page 103 on Gubbeen curing), the Cheddars are more dependent on the interior ripening controls that include flavour from the original milk and its butterfat, all of which are in turn influenced by the herd's feed.

For all cheese, as the microbial enzymes from the starter cultures break down the proteins, the depth of flavour increases. In some great Cheddars, as they age, you will find the effect of certain acids which form crystals. It is this chemistry, along with much, much more that brings us unique recognisable flavours.

The skill of the cheesemaker, and what makes a standard for their product, is in understanding the variables that produce the exact tone of flavour for a unique cheese, and then being able to repeat it accurately on a daily basis, as feed and climate perform subtle changes in the milk.

At Gubbeen we no longer have wooden shelving. Regulation was encroaching on us when we became involved in a programe that analysed our rinds and gave us the unique chance

of knowing the main active organisms that grew naturally in our Gubbeen Dairy. These we can now develop simply from a broth produced for us using the organisms in our curing rooms, and by washing them onto our rinds at the beginning of our curing process.

We are lucky the Gubbeen is similar to the great blue cheeses like Roquefort and Gorgonzola, which incorporated the native spores of the local caves and valleys into their taste range. Now, through scientific analysis, these spores have been identified and are managed as a business. You can buy them commercially, a little bit of the Gorgonzola, northern Italian hills' microbial history in a packet. Originally centuries old, they are now sold in a convenient packet that shares a taste with a unique meaning for us.

The great cheeses, like Parmigiano-Reggiano, aged for a full 12 months and more, are cured on by master graders who buy them from the farms and move them to their caves, their skills honed from generations of knowledge and learning. They use little hammers to tap the cheeses and, from the tones they hear, they can judge the quality and maturity of the cheese and gauge how long it needs before it is ready to sell.

It has taken centuries to acquire such skills and knowledge, and now, under the weight of so much food regulation, some of this ancient world has been threatened. We have visionaries in movements like Slow Food and the Soil Association to thank for publicising and lobbying for why we must protect our long-held farming and food traditions. When I meet certain young chefs I begin to feel the future is safe in their hands; and I am encouraged by support from food writers, researchers in university food departments and the shopping bags of the discerning public who believe authentic artisanal craft traditions stand for something as close to the human condition as any of the arts can be.

How to make Butter

Making your own butter is the easiest thing to do and will result in the most wonderful butter you will taste. All you need is to invest in a 500ml carton of single cream. As your butter will be made from pure cream it is going to have a higher fat count than shop-bought butter, so the taste will be sweeter.

I think that, with the growing number of dairies and specialist shops where you can buy milk and cream direct from a farm, you will readily be able to taste the differences of a single-herd unprocessed milk from the heat-treated homogenised version that is mass-produced for our convenience.

For me, the wonderful Channel Island breeds of cattle like Jersey and Guernsey produce cream that is just another thing altogether, golden and silky and addictively rich. Using milk from one breed or another gives subtle taste surprises, and this should be what dairying is all about. Try to track one down, or ask in a good grocer's shop where single farm cream can be found – it will be worth the effort and the extra pennies will be well spent when you taste it.

There is no trick to making butter; it is really simple – you are merely isolating the butterfat from the buttermilk by agitating it. So this recipe is for the fun of making it in your own home and having a small butter dish on your table with that obviously homemade look when friends come round. I know I would be seriously impressed if I was given 'my' butter.

I am sure that any commercially sold creams, including those from farms and single-breed herds as well as from supermarkets, are all pasteurised. If you can get raw cream from a neighbour or friend, please note the following: I have heard old dairying stories from France where the dairymen would draw off the raw cream and heat it to a good high temperature before adding it back to the milk as they believed the bacteria were caught in the heavy cream and this would destroy them, thus protecting their cheeses. I always listen to traditional advice as it is born out of observation that was handed down the generations.

We use raw cream from our herd for this butter for our family, but we would not sell it without it being tested first. Tom isolates the milk from our Jersey into a bucket, we let it settle overnight for the rich golden cream to rise, then skim it off. Tom knows she is very healthy and also not too close to having calved, so the cream will be good for butter.

Our butter days of long ago at Gubbeen took two forms: one for the family and another for the guests who came when Tom's mother ran Gubbeen as a farm guesthouse in the 60s. The cream for the guests' version would have been skimmed off the top of the churns that were kept cool in the stand on the north side of the yard waiting to go to the creamery. This would have been used for sweet butter made fresh in the kitchen, right up until the local creamery started a shop, then the local butter from Bandon would have taken its place; it also took all the work out of it!

In our grandparents' time butter was being made here regularly as there was none that was easily available locally. This would have been skimmed each day from the milk churns, then stored to 'ripen'. About a week's worth would be collected before being churned it into butter. During that week it would have been naturally growing some bacterial content and culture flavours. 'Country Butter' was preferred as it is quite rich-tasting with a little sharpness of acidity and a slightly flat but natural taste, and of course rather salty. I love to picture the butter being taken to Bantry fair wrapped in cabbage leaves to keep it cool. How beautiful that must have looked.

Cultured butter has a richer and slightly acidic edge to it, the 'buttery' aroma and notes coming from the diacetyl compound, a naturally occurring by-product of the fermentation process derived from certain lactic bacteria that you may have tasted in cultured cream or cultured buttermilk. In the same way that you can buy single-strain cheese cultures, you can also buy butter cultures. They are hard to find, though, so maybe trick the cream by adding a spoonful of cultured cream or buttermilk to steal its culture!

Quick Gubbeen Butter

EQUIPMENT
1-litre rubber-sealed jar
(be sure it has a wide neck)

MAKES 225–250G
(depending on your cream quality)

500ml single cream (close to its 'use by' date is good), not straight from the fridge, but not warm either
Salt (optional)

Pour the cream into the jar, which should be only half-full as once the cream starts to thicken it almost doubles in volume – you need 'shake room' in the jar right to the end. Be sure to seal it tightly and then simply roll and shake the jar for 15–30 minutes. As the cream starts to break down you will see it thicken and then separate.

Keep gently rolling and shaking for just a minute longer. At this point I sometimes tip it into a bowl as you can more easily watch the process, stirring it with a fork until the butter is free and the liquid is running clear (drain this into a jug, if you wish, for use in cooking – in Ireland it was always traditionally used to make soda bread), then gently wash the little butter beads in a sieve under cold water.

I love these tiny unpatted beads of butter, a bit like golden caviar. They have the nicest texture and can be added to your food in big generous spoonfuls or you can go on to the next stage: patting and salting.

Bring the butter together and handle it into a lump with cool hands (run them first under a cold tap) on a marble surface. Using butter pats, which are now quite easy to come by, or your flattest wooden spoon, start to pat it into shape. This drains off the last of the buttermilk, and that will ensure your butter has a longer shelf life. (If you find the butter sticks to the pats, soak them first in hot water and be sure the butter is cool enough to work.)

Butter pats have little grooves on them and the trick is to roll the butter into a cone up and down the pats, slightly squeezing it, then put it back down on the surface, flatten it out, then bring it together again.

Try the butter with no salt first – it is so delicious – but if you are a salt lover, add it at this stage, but very little (10g for 250g of butter), working it into the cool butter as you pat it. Repeat this several times to mix in the salt well, and you should have got rid of any excess moisture. The butter is ready.

My friend Lee suggests, instead of salt, adding anchovies or chopped seaweed – I am sure you can think of other things too, like spring herbs and cracked pepper.

Wrap it in greaseproof paper and it will keep in the fridge for several weeks, but, as I always say, why not just eat it?

How to Make Yogurt

To make yogurt you need a starter culture. These days there are many good sources for dried yogurt starter cultures available on the internet via mail order or from local suppliers. The strains originate from Scandinavia, Greece, Bulgaria, Georgia... wherever there are long traditions of yogurt eating. These cultures all produce a good yogurt and provide varying degrees of acidity and depth of flavour. All good yogurt cultures contain both *Streptococcus thermophilus* and *Lactobacillus bulgaricus*. Some have additional strains for texture and stronger flavours.

In the 'healthy eating' section of supermarkets you can find drinks boasting live pro-biotic strains that appear in our gut when we are truly healthy. These can be taken after a course of antibiotics to recolonise the gut, or simply to maintain a high number of good bacteria that our gut needs to function well. These are strains like *Lactobacillus acidophilus* and *Bifidobacterium animalis*, developed by microbiologists into foods that encourage good gut health. The single strains can be bought commercially to give the consumer the most virile and fast-acting acid production which is at the heart of good yogurt making. Some have richer softer flavours, others a big kick of acidity. Trying them out should be fun.

Gubbeen Yoghurt: Set and Thickened

We follow two basic yogurt recipes depending on how we are planning to use the finished product. The breakfast yogurt we love is a sharp clean-tasting 'set' yogurt that is simply made straight into a pot – it will perhaps show some whey at the edges after several days in the fridge, or if you spoon some out, this bleeding of whey is natural as the acidity expels it. This is a basic and very easy yogurt to make. Our second yogurt is the much heavier and protein-rich version that has a soft, smooth, thicker texture that works best in cooking as it stirs in, or may be substituted for sour cream if you prefer not to eat rich high fat too often.

VERSION 1 – SET YOGURT

EQUIPMENT

Stainless-steel bowl
Vacuum flask, or large lidded jar and bubble wrap
Dairy thermometer

MAKES 600ML

600ml whole milk, raw or pasteurised

For the yogurt starter culture

Small pinch of dried starter culture, or 2 teaspoons 'live' commercial yogurt
(We use a freeze-dried culture by Danesco called Yo-Mix 601, a good traditional yogurt culture from their range)

Note: Starter cultures for yogurt are designed to produce a nutritious and clean- and sharp-tasting yogurt. These are particular strains of lactobacilli with unique qualities for the best yogurt.

The raw milk will certainly have some other bacteria in it and even in small quantities these will compete with the starter cultures – so I suggest you heat-treat the milk first to clear any other bacteria away.

METHOD FOR HEAT-TREATING

Pour the milk into the stainless-steel bowl and place over a pan of water brought to a rolling boil. It is really important not to boil or scald the milk as this can give it a caramel flavour, which is not at all what you need with yogurt. Bring the milk temperature up to 85°C, then immediately cool it down to 40°C by putting the bowl of hot milk into a sink full of cold water. Stir gently until the milk temperature drops to just above 40°C.

Add your chosen starter and stir gently for several minutes. Pour into your flask, and place the lid on top but don't seal it shut – oxygen is needed for bacterial activity. Alternatively, pour the milk into the jar and wrap it well in bubble wrap, then store in a warm, clean place to set – again, put the lid on, but not sealed. This will take approximately 12 hours – warmer conditions will bring it in faster, but you might get a better flavour with the long slow set.

This is an almost full-proof system. You can of course use the yogurt you have just made to become the 'starter' for the next week's makes.

If you intend to make yoghurt regularly, I would go back now and then to the original culture source to be sure that you are growing the correct strains. It is all too easy to have one of the several strains dominate homemade yogurt, which can lead to dull flavours, or even to have a contamination that changes the texture.

This system will give you set yogurt – a lovely shiny, sharp-tasting curd with a sweet smell that makes your mouth water.

VERSION 2 – THICKENED YOGURT

This is the thicker or Greek-style yogurt. Once it is set, you stir it and then settle it back until it thickens well into the creamy form of yogurt that goes so beautifully with mixed fruit and so many recipes.

I have a trick that produces this for you without all the condensation and time that the original Greek system would have called for when you would 'reduce' the liquids in the milk with slow simmering until the solids were doubled.

Buy a tin of dried milk solids: Marvel is the best known and most readily available. Mix about 2 tablespoons of this powder into your heat-treated milk – you will be raising the proportion of milk solids, which means that your yogurt will be thick and creamier and it won't cut and release whey as a set yogurt does.

Add your starter in exactly the same way and store in a warm, clean environment as with set yogurt – you can stir this mixture after 12 hours and then leave it to set again into the nice thick consistency of Greek yogurt.

Both these yogurts can be kept in your fridge for about a week. They will store well in clean cartons, and now they can be lidded up for better storage.

Be wary of adding fruits that might have some bacteria in them, as certainly blackberries and garden raspberries will. This isn't a problem, of course, but if you want to add a layer at the bottom of your yogurt or mix them through the pot, make sure you store this yogurt for no more than 3 days. Even in your fridge, bacteria will multiply and you might get a fizzing effect in the yogurt.

If you feel that you would like to increase your knowledge of yogurt- or cheesemaking, see page 84.

Gubbeen Meltdown

Perfect for children home from school (minus the Kirsch) or, with the larger cheese, for a starving group home from the bar!

If you buy a small Gubbeen, which weighs approximately 450g, it will feed three children or two adults with a salad and crusty sourdough bread. The large Gubbeen is better suited for a party and will generally feed up to eight people.

SERVES 2–8

1 small (450g) or large (1.4kg) Gubbeen cheese
1 or 3 garlic cloves, thinly sliced
1 or 4 sprigs of thyme
1 or 2 sprigs of rosemary
50ml Kirsch for adults! (optional)
Freshly ground black pepper
Toasted Malthouse Sourdough (see page 232), to serve

Preheat the oven to 180°C/gas mark 4.

Select a suitable round ovenproof dish in which the Gubbeen will fit snugly (Spanish earthenware tapas dishes are perfect).

Slice through the equator of the cheese – this will create the lid and base. Place the garlic, thyme and rosemary across the cut side of the base of the cheese, add a twist of black pepper, then set the lid back on top.

Wrap the dish in a couple of folds of tinfoil, leaving a spout in the top, much like a pie hole, to release steam and stop the rind from splitting. Bake for 25–30 minutes for a small Gubbeen or up to 45 minutes for the large one – the principle being, cook till the cheese is molten!

When the cooking time is almost up, slice and toast the sourdough. Just before you tuck in, make a hole in the bubbling top of the cheese and pour in the Kirsch if you like. Serve with the toast and a green salad.

Potato Cakes & Soda Farls with Gubbeen Cheese

We first met Robert Ditty through our mutual respect for Slow Food, the organisation that champions locally produced food and regional cooking. Robert is one of Northern Ireland's best-known food producers, and his famous Ditty's Home Bakery in the village of Castledawson is legendary. Having survived against huge odds during the Troubles, it has grown as a result of his passion and skill.

Robert arrived at our farm after our meetings at Slow Food events. We spent a few hours talking about baking and cheeses and when he left we gave him a big smoked Gubbeen as a present. Two weeks later a parcel arrived from Belfast. In it were his wonderful Northern Oatcakes that he has made so famous and in these he had incorporated the smoked cheese we had given him… we have been in production together ever since!

These oatcakes are the product for which we get most 'fanmail' from people trying to find them in their corner of the world, asking for boxes to be sent to them. This is the result of two small food makers truly understanding what the origin of their work is – the land.

Potato Cakes

This is a classic food children absolutely love, the Potato Cake. When I think of these, I can smell the butter melting…

MAKES 6–8

EQUIPMENT
Cast-iron griddle

230g floury potatoes – often we use leftovers!
70g plain white flour
40g Gubbeen cheese, grated
12g butter, melted or olive oil
Salt

Peel the potatoes, cut into even-sized pieces and put into a pan of salted water. Bring to the boil, then simmer until cooked. Drain, mash and allow to cool.

Preheat a griddle or heavy-based pan (dust the griddle with a little flour – when the flour starts to colour, reduce the heat slightly and start baking).

Sift the flour with a pinch of salt and add to the cooled potatoes with the grated cheese and melted butter or olive oil. Knead into a dough. Divide into portions that suit your children's age and roll out into the required shapes. Place on the hot griddle (in batches if need be) and bake for about 3–4 minutes on one side before turning over and baking for another 3–4 minutes. Be careful not to let the cakes burn. Serve warm.

Tip: Fry the potato bread in a frying pan straight after you have cooked some bacon for extra flavour.

Soda Farls

MAKES 8
(OR 10 CANAPÉS)

EQUIPMENT
Cast-iron griddle

- 450g soda bread flour or self-raising flour, plus extra for dusting
- Pinch of salt
- 2 tablespoons vegetable oil
- 420–450ml buttermilk
- 200g Gubbeen cheese, grated

Preheat a griddle or heavy-based pan (dust the griddle with a little flour – when the flour starts to colour, reduce the heat slightly and start baking).

Sift the flour and salt several times into a large mixing bowl. Make a well in the middle and add the oil, buttermilk and the grated cheese and bring together with a spatula. Transfer to a flat surface dusted with flour and divide into two.

Knead each piece lightly into a round. Roll out to about 20cm diameter and cut into quarters. (Or, to make canapés, use a 2.5cm cutter or similar.)

Place on the hot griddle and bake for about 4 minutes on one side before turning over and baking for another 4 minutes. Repeat the process with the other piece of dough. Serve warm.

Mattie's Cauliflower and Gubbeen Ravioli

My friend Mattie cooks with such ease, his head over his shoulder. He is Italian and it is as easy as breathing for him. I went to lunch in his and Bertie's lovely hidden home, in a Suffolk wood, and the cheese I took him became this really special dish. I'm also grateful to Guillemette Barthouil from the Nordic Food Lab who cooked this beautiful dish for us on the day, also for the nice touch of adding butter-fried sage leaves!

SERVES 4 AS A STARTER OR 2 AS A MAIN DISH

1 free-range egg
100g '00' pasta flour
1 cauliflower head, cut into small florets
300g Gubbeen cheese, thinly sliced and cut into small squares (about 1½cm), plus extra, grated, to serve
Salt and freshly ground black pepper
Extra virgin olive oil, for drizzling
Gubbeen Cream (page 218), to serve (optional)
A few butter-fried sage leaves, to serve (optional)

Combine the egg and flour in a food processor, tip onto a clean, flat surface and work with your hands for 1–2 minutes until it forms a dough. (However, for this quantity you can easily do everything on a work surface and roll by hand if you don't have a food processor.) Wrap the dough in cling film and rest for 30 minutes. If you're not using the dough straight away, keep it wrapped in the fridge, but bring it back to room temperature before using as it will be much easier to roll out.

Steam the cauliflower until just tender. Leave a slight bite as the heat in the cauliflower means it will cook a little further after it's off the hob. Drain in a large colander, line a tray with a clean tea towel and lay the cauliflower on top – the towel will absorb any residual water. Allow to completely cool to room temperature.

Flour the work surface and roll out the pasta dough to the thickness of a penny (thinner if you can). Cut one long rectangular strip about 11–12cm in width. Brush the flour off the dough as best you can. Imagine a line down the centre from top to bottom. Your filling will occupy one side of that line.

Put a large pot of salted water on the hob and bring it to the boil. Place two squares of Gubbeen and a floret of cauliflower 2cm from the top edge and side of the pasta. Repeat every 6cm down its length, keeping to one side of that imaginary line. Frame each mound with a touch of water to help the pasta adhere. Fold the opposite side over and press gently between each mound with your fingers. Trim the edges with a pastry cutter or knife, then cut the ravioli into teabag-sized squares. Check each one and seal any gaps by pinching them together with your fingers.

Lower the pasta into the water with a slotted spoon. Check one after 2 minutes (chef's perk). If the pasta is giving and smoothing and the cheese has melted, the ravioli are ready. Remove them from the water using a slotted spoon and place in a colander quickly to drain off any excess water. Arrange on a plate and pour over some Gubbeen Cream and add the sage leaves, if using, or grate some parmesan on top. Drizzle with olive oil and add a good grind of black pepper. Serve immediately, nice and hot.

Gubbeen Cheese & Chorizo Potato Cake with Wilted Chard

Having a wonderful café so near us in Durrus is a blessing. Carmel Somers is a genuine menu genius; she has a huge knowledge of flavours and comes up with natural and delicious combinations, which makes a trip to The Good Things Café such a treat; it's an education each time we go. Carmel uses sea cabbage, which grows on the strand in front of her café, but we always use chard.

SERVES 2

Splash of olive oil, plus extra for frying
Knob of butter
500g peeled potatoes
100g smoked Gubbeen cheese, grated
100g Gubbeen chorizo, sliced
2 big handfuls of chard
4 free-range eggs
Salt and freshly ground black pepper

Preheat the oven to 200°C/gas mark 6.

Heat a 20cm frying pan on a medium heat, then melt together a good splash of oil and a knob of butter, coating the bottom and the sides of the pan with the mixture. Pour off any excess fat and keep in a bowl until later.

Lower the heat and start slicing the potatoes – they need to be very thin, but not so thin that you don't get a complete slice. Layer the potatoes in the pan in a clockwise direction, starting from the outside and working your way into the middle, making sure you are spreading them evenly leaving no gaps. Season with salt and pepper about every third layer.

When you have layered half the potato, top with the cheese and chorizo, then continue layering the potatoes. You want to finish with a nice thick cake, so there is a contrast of crisp and soft potato. Add another potato if you think it's needed! Brush the top with the reserved oil mixture, place in the middle of the oven and bake for 20–30 minutes until the potatoes are soft when tested with a knife.

If the top of the cake is not nice and brown, flip the cake out onto a plate or chopping board, slide back, topside down, into the pan and either return to the oven or cook on the hob on a medium heat for a few minutes.

In the meantime, cook the chard in boiling water and drain well. Heat some olive oil in a frying pan and fry the eggs.

Turn out the cake onto a plate or chopping board, cut into wedges and serve with the chard and fried eggs.

Cynthia's Kefir Drop Scones

Cynthia looks after everything and everyone in the smokehouse. She brings treats in for her boys most weeks, and this recipe is a favourite and really worth making: the scones are just amazing. Her secret is using kefir, a wonderfully strange milk product that comes from 'grains' of lactic bacteria and yeasts that are bound together with proteins that look a bit like cauliflower florets. Added to milk, they bring out really intense acidification, resulting in a viscous and wickedly strong drinking yogurt. It is available either from good health-food shops as a starter kit, or from friends with their own grains that have multiplied and been shared out. Kefir is extremely good for you – I think this is lactic Dyno-rod, driving the pH down right along your gut!

These drop scones are wonderful with butter and honey, or try serving them like blinis with sour cream, chopped onion and smoked salmon. We like them with Grüne Soße (see page 209).

If you can't find Cynthia's magic ingredient, you can substitute a sharp yogurt for the kefir.

MAKES 24 SMALL DROP SCONES

225g self-raising flour
175ml kefir
1 free-range egg
Pinch of salt
Melted butter, for frying

Combine all the ingredients apart from the butter and whisk until smooth. Leave to stand in the fridge for 30 minutes. Bubbles will appear in the mixture.

Heat a pancake pan or frying pan and lightly coat with melted butter. Drop dessertspoonfuls of the batter into the pan and cook for 1–2 minutes, or until bubbles appear and pop. Flip over and cook on the other side until brown. Cool a little on a wire rack and serve warm.

Vanilla Ice Cream

Freshly churned ice cream on a warm summer night, or when a child comes in with that need for something special! It is so simple with a machine and really not hard if you make it by hand, but be sure to take the nearly frozen mixture out and stir vigorously to break up the ice crystals. These are some of our favourite flavours.

MAKES **1.5** LITRES

600ml full-cream milk
2 vanilla pods, split
8 free-range egg yolks, beaten
300g sugar
600ml double cream

Pour the milk into a high-sided pan. Scrape out the vanilla seeds and add them and the pods to the milk and slowly bring to the boil, stirring occasionally. As soon as it boils remove from the heat, cover and allow to infuse for 20 minutes.

Whisk the egg yolks and sugar in another pan until pale and frothy. Remove the vanilla pods (they still have some flavour, so rinse and dry them and put them into your sugar jar to make vanilla-infused sugar) and whisk the infused milk into the egg mixture, then put the pan over a low heat and stir until the custard has thickened and will coat the back of a spoon. Leave to cool and then add the cream.

Churn in an ice-cream machine for about 15–20 minutes until softly frozen, then scoop it out with a spatula into tubs. Freshly churned ice cream straight from the machine truly is something to behold. Store and that isn't eaten immediately in the freezer.

VARIATIONS
Following the same recipe, you can replace the vanilla pods with all sorts of other good things. Here are some suggestions.

Hazelnut Ice Cream

Use the same ingredients as for Vanilla Ice Cream (above), but omit the vanilla pods and use 250g hazelnuts, toasted and skinned. Put the cooled nuts in a food processor or use a pestle and mortar to coursely grind them. Combine with the milk in a high-sided pan and slowly bring to the boil. As soon as it boils remove from the heat, cover and allow to infuse for 1 hour or more. Strain the milk through a sieve, discarding the hazlenuts.

Whisk the egg yolks and sugar in another pan until pale and frothy. Whisk the infused milk into the egg mixture, then put the pan over a low heat and stir until the custard has thickened and will coat the back of a spoon. Leave to cool, then add the cream.

Churn in an ice-cream machine for about 15–20 minutes until softly frozen, then scoop it out with a spatula into tubs and store in the freezer.

Cold-filtered Coffee Ice Cream

Cold-filtered coffee has a lower acidity than the ordinary filtered sort because it never comes into contact with hot water, which means the sweeter notes of coffee are more pronounced. To my mind, this makes it more suitable for using in ice cream.

Use the same ingredients as for Vanilla Ice Cream (opposite) but omit the vanilla pods and use 100g coarsely ground coffee. Add the coffee to 500–600ml full-cream milk, stir well and allow to sit in a cool room for as long as you can wait: overnight or for 12–24 hours. Stir occasionally to help the infusion.

Strain the coffee grinds from the milk through a very fine sieve or a paper coffee filter into a measuring jug. Top up the milk quantity with fresh full-cream milk to 600ml.

Whisk the egg yolks and sugar in another pan until pale and frothy. Whisk the infused milk into the egg mixture, then put the pan over a low heat and stir until the custard has thickened and will coat the back of a spoon. Leave to cool and then add the cream.

Churn in an ice-cream machine for about 15–20 minutes until softly frozen, then scoop it out with a spatula into tubs and store in the freezer.

Salted Liquorice Ice Cream
(Good Things Café, Durrus)

MAKES **1.5** LITRES

600ml full-cream milk
3–4 bars of Panda brand liquorice, chopped
8 free-range egg yolks
200g sugar
600ml double cream
Salt, to taste

Pour the milk into a high-sided pan, add the chopped liquorice and slowly bring to the boil, stirring occasionally to discourage the liquorice from sticking to the bottom. As soon as it boils remove from the heat, cover and allow to infuse for 20 minutes.

Whisk the egg yolks and sugar in another pan until pale and frothy. Whisk the infused milk into the egg mixture, then put the pan over a low heat and stir until the custard has thickened and will coat the back of a spoon. Leave to cool and then add the cream and the salt to your taste. Once the ice cream has frozen, the salt flavour will have mellowed, so you may need to add a little more than you think.

Churn in an ice-cream machine for about 15–20 minutes until softly frozen then scoop it out with a spatula into tubs and store in the freezer.

Carrigeen Pudding

Tom grew up eating carrigeen, the red seaweed that grows down on the strand here, just below the tidemark. We pick it from just under the water and dry it well. This is one of my favourite desserts, and we do have it often, but you can change the fruits you serve with it to suit the season.

Adding the orange and marmalade, as in this recipe, is to make it a warm winter pudding: the cardamom spiciness and orange are great companions in a milky pudding.

SERVES 6

990ml full-cream milk
A semi-closed fistful of clean, dry carrigeen (about 7–8g)
Grated zest of 2 large unwaxed oranges
6 green cardamom pods
2 tablespoons honey, or to taste.
Marmalade, to serve

Combine all the ingredients (apart from the marmalade) in a pan and bring gently to the boil, being careful not to scorch the milk. Simmer for 20 minutes.

Strain through a sieve into a serving bowl or into pretty glasses for dinner, if you like. Cover and chill until it has a tantalising wobble when jiggled.

Serve with a generous blob of marmalade.

Cardamom Shortbread

We find these shortbread biscuits make a wonderful contrast to the Carrigeen Pudding.

MAKES A 25CM TART/16 PIECES

355g plain flour, sifted
230g cold unsalted butter, diced
155g unrefined caster sugar, plus 1 tablespoon for sprinkling
8 green cardamom pods, crushed in a pestle and mortar, husks removed

Preheat the oven to 160°C/gas mark 3.

Put the flour, butter, sugar and cardamom in a large bowl and start working everything together with your hands. Rub the mix between your fingertips and hands – don't be shy about this – and you'll notice that it starts to look a lot like breadcrumbs. Keep mixing and rubbing until the shortbread is just incorporated into one smooth mass.

Pack the shortbread evenly into a 25cm tin and bake in the oven for 20–25 minutes until it has a hint of colour and is dry and crunchy. Remove the tin from the oven, sprinkle with caster sugar and allow to cool for 10 minutes on a wire rack to firm up.

Take a sharp knife and cut the shortbread into your desired number of portions: sixteen is a good number. It's important to do this while the shortbread is still warm otherwise it becomes too brittle to cut.

The beauty of shortbread is that it keeps so well, stored in an airtight tin.

Pure Drinking Chocolate

When our family was young we shared many adventures and projects with William Harcourt-Cooze, Clovisse's godfather, a man who always brought adventure into every project we shared. He owned Horse Island and farmed sheep and later cattle there. Picnics on this tiny windswept island were always times of complete freedom. He and his wonderful family enriched all those around them and now William's son, Willie Harcourt-Cooze, whose childhood years were spent on Horse Island, is following very much in his father's visionary ways, running Willie's Cacao, a business selling world-class eating chocolate. Willie's name was familiar when he became the subject of a Channel 4 television series, Willie's Wonky Chocolate Factory. *His company produces truly top-quality chocolate using the very finest beans sourced from his own farm in Venezuela and from single-farm producers in Cuba, Peru, Madagascar and Indonesia.*

We always have in our cupboards the big 180g cylinders of Willie's grating chocolate. The products in the range all provide a unique taste experience: new, very individual, intense flavours of 100 per cent pure cacao. Grating it into warmed fresh milk is a wonderful winter thing!

SERVES 2

2 cups milk
2 tablespoons grated 100 per cent pure cacao chocolate from Willie's Cacao range (and why not 3 tablespoons?)
Cane sugar, to taste
Irish whiskey, to serve (optional)

Warm the milk in a saucepan. Stir in the grated cacao chocolate and stir constantly until it is melted. Sweeten to taste. On a freezing night why not add a tot of good Irish whiskey? Not for the children, of course!

4

The Smokehouse

EACH of the foods we make here at the Smokehouse comes from a variety of influences. Different people and different countries have played a part in my becoming a charcutier. Of course, the first influences were here at my home, Gubbeen. Earliest memories are hard to keep in order, but certainly they must have started around our kitchen table. It's the centre of the house, where we all ate at least three times a day during my childhood. For big events like birthdays and Christmas we would move out of the kitchen into the dining room, but to be honest that always involved good behaviour and table manners – not half as much fun as in the kitchen.

It's a real farmhouse kitchen, a large square room with black beams, an Aga and dogs – always dogs: under the table, in the seats, at the door. The walls are white and from the beams hang herbs, hats, onions, garlic and (for some reason best known to my mother) a huge padlock. The long pine table has benches down both sides and two chairs at each end; this is the table where food is prepared and where we all eat. It is where the family still meets to talk, and where we all still eat together, at least once a day.

My Dad, Tom, like his father, loves beef, so as a boy I remember we would fatten our own animals and carry them to the slaughterhouse, which at that time was up on a hill above the farm. There they were slaughtered, and back we would come to fill up the freezer. The roasts were always special – perhaps it's the Aga, with its intense burst of heat to seal in the flavours. Those childhood roast potatoes were something special, well worth fighting over. The kitchen table was of course also the place for great food debates, one being what was the right moment for beef to be taken out of the oven. My mother, Giana, also comes from a kitchen culture, though a more European one, where meat was served pink, and so deciding on the timing for the perfect colour and gravy was nerve-wracking. It wasn't until the day Tom found a meat thermometer that a truce was forged, and the beef could come out to rest.

Chicken too – there is a long tradition of Sunday chicken in this house, though it could happen on any day, not necessarily just Sunday. As ravenous teenagers this meant entering into our own dreadful pecking order of who gets the breast and who gets the bones, negotiating which piece is biggest and which is smallest, and who takes precedence. When I was young these table birds came from a friend in Durrus and were perfect, with the delicious flavours of a farm-reared chicken that has fed and exercised well, so the meat is firm. There was a period when we would buy tasteless, commercially reared birds, and I think this put us off chicken for a while. Giana did rear some now and then and Tom, always called in to be executioner, would sit up in the Haggard plucking them – not a job I was too fond of. I think one of the first things

I ever cooked was chicken liver pâté from these chickens.

Since the farmers' markets have developed, we again have the best chickens from a very dedicated friend, David Louks, who rears and feeds his birds with great care and skill. Buying one of his birds involves negotiation: he wants to hear how it's going to be cooked and who will eat it, and each week he comes by and asks, 'Was it good? Did you enjoy it?' Dave and I have the same approach to the foods we make. We send them off into the world in the hope that they are going to make someone's dinner special, that they are truly enriching our customers' lives.

Family life was full of food rituals, but my favourite involved 'the family knife'. In my grandfather's day this knife was used to kill the pigs, back when they were slaughtered here on the farm. In my childhood we used it to cut the bread each morning for breakfast toast and, on Sundays, wielded by Tom, it would carve the chicken or the beef for the family dinner. It's a lovely old wooden-handled knife with a long black carbon-steel blade with a rounded tip – I wonder if this is a West Cork-style blade, not often seen these days. It has an ability to take an edge, the secret being not only in the quality of the steel but also in Tom's habit of taking it outside just beyond the kitchen door, as the meat came to the table, and honing it up and down on the fine sand-plastered wall. That noise was the best call to table there was.

Food has a central place in our family, with storing and planning always essential from one season to another, as it is on most farms, for the likes of summer puddings made for Christmas Day, as well as jams and jellies, mushrooms and fish. Many summer evenings I would come in to find Tom gutting a sinkful of fish from a doctor friend who loved sea fishing; great big buckets of herring or mackerel would arrive, still stiff after one of his fishing trips.

The whole kitchen is endlessly taken over with these sorts of projects. It was all really exciting as a child, and with Tom and Giana talking about how to cook these harvests for dinner that night it gave you a lovely sense of anticipation for the meal to come.

Throughout my childhood the Dairy grew and grew, and it was when I was a teenager, at the time we began to produce smoked cheese, that I met someone who would help me form my own food plans, Chris Jepson; he was to be another big influence on my ideas.

I think what impressed me most about Chris was that he did things in his own individual way. One of the first salmon smokers in West Cork, he built his business with ingenious independence. He made his own boat to catch salmon and smoked them in a smokehouse he built himself. When he couldn't find the tools he needed to cut and lay hedges, he made them in his own little forge. To me this was an inspiration: why let the lack of equipment stop your plans? Make it yourself.

So it was that Chris became an integral part of making the smoked cheese. It was real teamwork. Giana would make the cheeses here in our dairy and we would load them into clean white trays. Tom and I would drive the cheeses over to Goleen, down to the little bay. We would park the van at the water's edge and carry them over the strand and up the steep beach to Chris's smokehouse. The cheeses were slotted on their trays into shelving in this dark, smoky room at the edge of Chris's house and left there for four days to absorb the flavour of the oak smoke. Tom always knew when the tide was out, but once I had learnt to drive I would inevitably leave it to the last second and get to the strand just as the tide was nearly in. This meant I had to wade across to the smokehouse, and one day I slipped, sending the tray into the air. I went down into the water and when I resurfaced there were cheeses floating all around me – another one of those lessons.

It was the smoker that fascinated me most. Chris had learnt the system from the famous salmon smokers Pinney's of Orford, in Suffolk, who operated a system using a steel smoking barrel that smouldered down pieces of hardwood. Not only did Chris teach me how to build and work a smoker, but it was also in his smokehouse that I first tasted home-cured bacon.

The roots of all this had started for me much earlier, however, through another influence, my grandfather Peter. He was a writer who lived in Spain up a mountain in Andalucia, and many great holidays were spent with him and the rest of my mother's large and very colourful family when I was small. We went to Ronda and Malaga and small villages where great jamóns were sliced with respect and appreciation. To a young boy from West Cork the tastes and smells of a perfect jamón or chorizo and a glass of chilled fino sherry were inspiring, the stuff of dreams.

As soon as I got home from New Zealand, where I was completing my Agricultural Certificate, smoking was the skill that really took hold in my mind as a fascinating and valuable way to potentially make a living on our farm. With Gubbeen under my boots, Chris Jepson's smoking skills in my head, and the memory of Spanish meats lingering in my memory, I had the makings of a plan.

One early step took me back to Spain. I was invited by Darina Allen to meet the Chestertons on their farm Finca Buenvino near Aracena in Andalucia. This gave me the opportunity to go to a *matanza*, the Andalucian tradition of pig-killing and curing held in the cold months of November. A *matanza* begins with the ceremonial slaughter of the pigs. Neighbours and relatives then work together in the process of making the traditional foods: jamón, lomo, chorizo, pancetta and salchichon. Then come the feasting and drinking over a couple of days when the entire community congregates – with Sam and Jeannie Chesterton this was an experience that set me on a road and really deeply impressed my feeling for this work.

Around the same time, Giana had become wholly dedicated to the Slow Food movement. She worked with many of West Cork's great foodmakers running Slow Food Ireland events all over the place at a period when there really was nothing like this happening in our country – little local events in pubs and on beaches to celebrate our local foods – growing our food culture into a movement. This movement became a sort of national food identity, and it was soon clear that Slow Food Ireland was here to stay.

The first big, ground-breaking event was when Giana and a great friend, Clodagh McKenna, dreamed up a mad project: why not take over a local hotel for one weekend and go national – invite all the key artisan food makers, along with the food regulators, for a huge celebration of West Cork's meat, fish, breads, butter, game, cheeses and, of course, music and talk. It was an enormous undertaking, and they must have worked for weeks planning it with Darina and their sponsors. I remember one thing – that was that noone said 'no' to them. Everyone seemed to share the vision, everyone wanted to join in and help.

That night three waiters led by a bodhrán player brought an enormous tabletop of oysters for 200 people into a room lit by candles, and I think everyone present realised that Irish food was changing forever. Late that same night I saw Giana making paella in the kitchen with one of the heads of the Food Safety Authority, and it became clear as well that the Slow Food principle of 'conviviality' was taking the Irish artisan food movement into a whole new relationship with regulators.

The weekend ended with an outdoor farmers' market, so as the guests left for home they could take with them the homemade bread and cheeses, eggs from farm-raised chickens, and locally cured bacon and sausages. It may very well have been the moment when many markets were born; but that's another story…

Slow Food soon lured me out to Italy, to Salone del Gusto in Turin; it was a paradise for a young artisan foodmaker. I met people and foods there, some with traditions literally dating back to hunter-gatherers. It was there I encountered some of the greatest meat curers in the world and saw the standards I was to work for once I started on my own small business back home. This too was certainly another of the great inspirations for me.

So this was the challenge, for a young farmer in West Cork, with our admittedly great pork, to create a new taste here at home with fermented meats. I had the belief that if I loved my products, others would too, and through study and the help of Spanish and Italian masters in the field the potential was there to make Irish cured meats with our very own signature flavours that, like Giana's cheeses, came from our climate and the land here at Gubbeen.

The Pigs and the Process

The Gubbeen pigs are a particular selection of breeds that include Saddleback, Tamworth, Duroc, Large White and Gloucester. We make this selection both because of a nostalgic connection to the older breeds and also because of their superior flavour. The type of products we make also requires a certain amount and quality of fat, so we are not afraid of using the older breeds that more commercial operations might be wary of using because of their fat layers.

With our own farm-reared pigs and the outdoor reared pork that we buy we produce the majority of our products, such as the bacon, hams and salamis. Due to peaks in demand we have always had to buy in locally sourced commercial loins and belly at these times (which we label). The focus of our future plans is the pig co-operative will fill this gap with well-reared farm pork.

Our piggery consists of big straw pens in a large barn, open along one side to the land and fresh air, unlike commercial units where the buildings are heated in order to grow the pigs faster. We believe that if you rush a pig you end up with very soft, wet meat, whereas a rare-breed pig, reared in a well-ventilated area, grows more slowly, giving redder, firmer meat with harder fat, and this is what we are looking for.

Our pigs grow on here until six to eight months of age, depending on time of year and breed, at which point they go off to O'Donoghue's Slaughterhouse about 8 miles away from our farm. At present we process about twelve pigs a week, on occasion buying in from a few neighbouring farms who rear their pigs to the same standard.

At O'Donoghue's the pigs are put in pens where they fast for 24 hours and are checked by a vet. Then, without being put through any stress, they are stunned and slaughtered, and each pig is bled while its heart is still beating, which is a vital part of the slaughter process. They are then gutted and hung in cold rooms. Two days later we return to the slaughterhouse to split the carcasses; we use a cleaver as it gives a cleaner cut than a saw, which can smear the carcass. At this stage they are checked again by a vet, who will takes samples to test for trichinella, a parasite that luckily for us is not in this country, and one we want to make sure is kept out. The sides are then returned to the Smokehouse where they hang over the weekend in preparation for butchering on the following Monday.

Hang a pig for too long, and it will begin to dry out. One per cent of the pig's moisture disappears every day it hangs in refrigeration. We find a drier pig is not good for our curing process; two or three

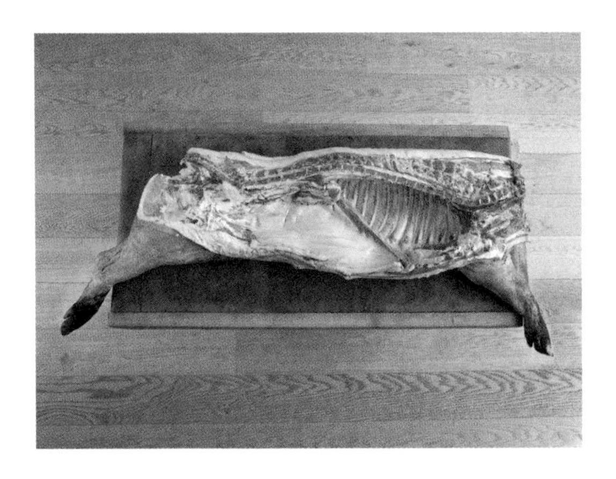

days' hanging is about perfect, making it easy to butcher and skin.

For Monday butchering we separate the carcasses into loins, belly, shoulders, ribs, fillets, sausage meat and salami meat, and put each cut into its own tub. Our pork cuts get tied up handsomely for the farmers' markets, as do the ribs and the fillets, and the loins and bellies are set aside for dry curing. Then comes the interesting part: dividing up salami meat and sausage meat. For this we use a visual process, working out the meat-to-fat ratio (which is about 3:1 or 4:1 depending on the type of salami being made). We avoid any gristle and sinew as we're looking for the higher-end cuts from the shoulder meat. About 25 per cent of a pig is waste – the skin and bones, gristle and sinew. It's one of the highest percentages, aside perhaps from that of chicken, but being such a meat-producing animal it maintains its popularity.

On Tuesday we cure the loins and the legs; as the cuts come out of the curing vessels we wash off all excess salt and brine, tie them up and hang them on our racks to rest for about 24 hours, after which they can be portioned, sliced, diced or smoked. Once we know exactly how much salami and sausage we're making to suit the week's orders, we can make our spice blends to match. In the afternoon we make our fresh sausage, putting our tubs of pork with whatever salt and spices are

needed into a big mixing and mincing machine. The meats are well chilled, so on Wednesday we take this chilled sausage meat and pack the filling machine. Once made, the sausages are linked and packed. Working with sausage meat is a relatively simple process, though our sausages are closer in style to continental ones than to the traditional Irish sausage as they contain sundried tomato, basil and garlic, or, for Italian sausage, lots of ground fennel seed and pepper.

When the sausages are made, we get the mixes and blends ready for the salamis, which will marinate for the next 48 hours in the cold room in preparation for finishing off the process later in the week.

On Thursday, we slice the meats from the blast chiller into bacon rashers, which is pretty much a full day's work. We've found that the easiest way to slice bacon is by tempering it, which involves lowering the temperature of the blaster to more than -11°C overnight. This makes the cuts firm but not frozen, much easier to slice cleanly. A sideline from the sliced bacon is lardons, which are diced by hand and use all the ends that are not packaged for bacon.

By Friday we are nearly finished, with just the salamis to make. This has become the focus of our production and is where so much work and research has been done, and it is probably our main product at this time of writing.

Salamis and Chorizo

For me, chorizo comes under the heading of salami. We have always made it; the very first product I ever did was a chorizo. I made a small batch at around the same time that I dry cured some bacon the way Chris Jepson showed me, and it triggered a nostalgic connection with my grandfather's way of life in Spain – those big flavours that fascinated me at a younger age were all there in the chorizo.

There are various types of salami, all of which undergo a form of fermentation. You could either use the lactic cultures that are naturally present in the air and on the meat itself, which is a rather random approach, or, if you want consistency, you buy them from suppliers like Danisco or CHR Hansen, amongst others, who produce these cultures as freeze-dried sachets. Each variety has its own distinctive properties: some are fast acting, others are slower; some will produce a higher acidity while others give your meat a redder colour. These ingredients are for a specialised sector in the meat industry and of course they would supply you with advice and guidelines if you needed to research the best cultures to use.

In our production, after checking the meat-to-fat ratio, we decide whether we want a more fatty salami, like chorizo (about three parts meat to one part fat) or a leaner one, like pepperoni (about four parts meat to one part fat). Then we take our meat, hand cut it, dice it, put it through the mincer on the coarsest plate we have and then we weigh everything into 20-kilo tubs. This way we can more accurately prepare our freshly ground spice mixes, which we make on the same day.

One trick for mincing is to take the meat after it has been cut up and put it in the freezer for a couple of hours before you mince it. This gives you a really clean cut through the fat. If you try to make salami without chilled meat you won't get as good a result, as the fat gets mashed around and makes the salami greasy, not least because the mechanical process of mincing raises the temperature of the meat by a couple degrees. Ideally, you want to do your mincing with the meat below 7°C.

We chill the meat again after mincing, then we add to the mince an appropriate amount of lactic cultures along with unchlorinated water at around body temperature, which wakes up the freeze-dried cultures, making them multiply like crazy. All of this is done before we have added any salt or other ingredients. Salt inhibits the activity of cultures, and as their fermentation is the building block for flavour you want to let them get a foothold first.

About an hour later we add in the pre-weighed spice blends, still keeping everything as cold as possible. Using a paddle mixer we mix for about 5 minutes and then the meat goes back into its tub and is patted down. This goes into a cold room for 48 hours, after which we either mince again or, for a coarser salami, fill the meat straight into a salami casing (depending on the type of salami being made).

There are several kinds of casing to work with, all available in different diameters and sizes. Note that the bigger the casing, the longer the salami takes to dry; the smaller it is, the sooner it is ready. We use our big powerful filler powered by a vacuum to stuff the meat into the casing and then tie it off. This process prevents the meat from developing air bubbles, which would cause spoilage. In a small batch, working without a vacuum, you could always prick the salamis multiple times with a needle and squeeze any air out.

Once they are in their casing we hang the salamis on hooks or sticks in our incubation room (which in our case is also our smoker), where there is a heater with a thermostat. We want the

room temperature to be about 27°C, and because of the size of the room – about 3.5 by 3 metres – it takes a while to bring the heat up. This gentle raising of the temperature starts the fermentation process: the meat and the cultures begin to feed off the dextrose or on the natural sugars present in the meat.

Increasing the temperature also encourages the cultures to multiply once more, producing lactic acid and lowering the pH of the meat. It starts to bond and bind the meat too, and, of course, help it to achieve that all-important fermented flavour. Humidity is another vital factor. If your room is too dry, you get 'case hardening', which is when the outside casing of the salami becomes like a piece of leather, so it will not be able to shrink with the salami as it starts to age, making the salami appear to become hollow and badly textured. We want the salami to lose about a third of its weight, and for the casing to shrink with it in a good even contact with the filling. Humidity is maintained very simply by putting a bucket of warm water on the floor of the smoker for 24 hours of this incubation stage; humidity can be reduced just by letting some fresh air into the room. You are looking for the surface of the meat to feel neither wet nor dry to the touch.

At this point, I introduce the smoker into the room. The kiln smoulders overnight, releasing the flavours of the wood, and the next day the salamis are ready. They can now come straight out of the smoker and be hung in our maturation room which we keep at 15°C with a humidity of 70–77 per cent, until the salamis lose a third of their weight.

Nitrates

Nitrates, or curing salts, are present in a lot of foodstuffs naturally, especially leafy green vegetables – they're a part of our life. A potassium nitrate or a sodium nitrate will break down to become nitric oxide, and in the meat-curing industry they do a number of beneficial things: they give you that familiar flavour and tang, slow down the formation of rancid and sour flavours, bind with the myoglobin in meat to maintain colour and kill pathogenic airborne spores.

There are different curing salts available for different jobs. Some contain only nitrite (a simpler form of nitrate) and others are a combination of nitrate and nitrite. A curing salt containing nitrate is used for slower, longer-cured products such as salamis and air-dried hams. Those with only nitrite are used for products with a quicker process. The slower breakdown of nitrates produces a small amount of nitrite to improve the shelf life and enhance flavour.

Under certain circumstances, nitrates can produce nitrosamines, which are undesirable, so it's important not to add more curing salts than required. Adding ascorbic acid (vitamin C) helps to reduce nitrosamines and also enhances the effects of nitrites. With modern regulation, though, you will only find low amounts of nitrites in any well-made products.

Fermentation and Food Safety for Salamis

If raw salami mix was brought up to 75°C, you would know it was safe to eat. As we don't cook our salamis we rely on fermentation. There are three important elements here that support safety: the drying out of the meat, the salt content and the pH or acidity. Having all these hurdles monitored carefully and working for us in harmony is what we want to achieve.

Our maturation room is humidity- and temperature-controlled in a similar way to curing rooms for cheeses. It should be neither too cold, so that the fermentation stops, nor so hot that the salamis sweat. I like it to be around 12–15°C, and the humidity should be set to about 77 per cent. This will support the salamis as they lose the necessary third of their weight, and depending on their diameter this can take from 14 days to a month. You can judge whether the salami is ready with experience by feeling their firmness with your hand, or, if you are new to the game, you can just weigh them. We do a quick check of the pH before the batch goes out, and carry out monthly product testing for taste as well as the bacteriology to make sure everything is just right.

We plan for them to have a good shelf life, too. Our vacuum-packed salamis have been shown to last for about 80 days. They can last a lot longer in ideal conditions, but be warned: they might start to lose their colour and then the flavours will begin to fall off too.

For moulded salami we make one variation, a tweak to the process. Once we've filled the salamis into their casings and before we put them into the incubation room to heat them, we inoculate them with a liquid solution of a surface bloom. Again, you can either buy these cultures or let the natural flora grow, but to avoid hit-and-miss batches I'd recommend the former. I use *Penicillium nalgiovense*, but you can also use *Penicillium candidum*, which is the same bloom that grows on Brie and gives you a white velvety mould on the surface.

Our system is to add a sachet to a bucket of unchlorinated water and leave it overnight, then dunk the salamis into the solution to seed the outside completely with the culture bloom; they are then hung in an incubation room with high humidity (about 85 per cent) and a higher temperature (20–25°C). The bloom will start to grow in about four days and should then take over the surface. Once the colonies start to show around day 3, we ease down the temperature to about 12°C and change the humidity to 77 per cent. These conditions will nurture the bloom into slowly taking over.

The mould has various roles. As it stakes its claim over the entire surface of the salami it wards off any undesirable airborne bacteria. As a good bloom it then creates a seal, retaining the moisture in the salami. The roots (mycelium) of the bloom inside the salami contribute texture as well as introducing enzymes that break down the meat and introduce flavours – a similar process to what happens on the surface of rind-washed cheese.

A moulded salami is a different animal from a smoked one. We keep them in a room with higher humidity and less air movement. You can allow some air circulation, but not the use of a powerful fan as you would with smoked salami, as this would dry out the surface. Moulded salamis do take a little bit longer to mature and air-dry but you are rewarded with a different, softer taste and texture, and a more exciting balance of flavours than you get with smoked salamis, which have a consistent sharpness and firmness.

Just as Giana has taken years exploring the rinds of her cheeses, I imagine I will spend years experimenting with the maturation of my salamis – testing flavours and ageing processes until, hopefully, I will arrive at the exact taste and texture that will represent the Gubbeen Smokehouse.

Bacon and Ham

There are two ways of curing meat. The first is by brining, often called pickling, and the second is by what is known as 'dry curing', achieved by the direct rubbing in of salts and sugars. Both methods of course have one essential ingredient: salt. Most people use a 'curing salt', a sodium nitrite or nitrate or a potassium nitrite or nitrate. Both are very similar and both achieve the same thing, which is to give cured meats their particular tang.

As far back as Roman times there would have been naturally occurring nitrates in the salt used to preserve meat. In some areas, the salts would have had higher proportions of naturally occurring nitrate and it would have become apparent that this gave better results. Of course with modern food technology these ingredients and their specific functions are analysed, so instead of using saltpetre (potassium nitrate) we now have a quicker form of this nitrate, which is nitrite. Potassium nitrate breaks down to become potassium nitrite during the curing process and becomes a nitric oxide. This kills off pathogens and preserves the meats, but, more important, it creates the 'cured' flavour we love, and it also gives the meat a red colour.

I grew up with brining in West Cork, where every butcher's shop you went into would have a barrel in the back of the cold rooms with big lumps of meat and crubeens (pigs' feet) floating in it. These brines are fantastic sources for the originality and character of flavour as well as acting as a preservative, just as traditional brine baths do with cheese.

There is a part of me that loves the romance of the stories you hear about old brine vats. Add to this the 'magic', or the unique flora of an old, complex brine and all its activity, and you've got the reason, I think, why Ireland became so famous for its ham.

These days, with risk assessment and food regulations, I feel we rely more perhaps on spices and herbs, or smoking, for the individuality of flavour. In the early days there would have been a tolerance for a higher salt content. The charcutier's skill is to get the balance right: too much salt means the meat will be loaded (or 'lit' in Irish!) with this flavour; too little and it will be lacking in flavour and, worse, the meat may spoil. Getting this right is absolutely one of the most important parts of the process.

Good-quality meat and gentle brining are the two other most important factors for a really great ham. We of course rigorously check our mixes with brinometers to give ourselves the proper information and control we need, and we have also invested in a brine pump, a hollow needle that helps inject the salts right down into the bone area of a big pork leg, preventing spoilage.

Taking a well-butchered ham, weigh it and calculate the exact amount of salt needed, then inject that into the meat, vacuum pack it and leave it for a specific period of time – in our case about six days, depending on size. After that open the pack, pour off the excess brine and tie it up to hang in a cold room. You can then portion it or smoke it or do whatever the customers want.

For extra character you can infuse and influence the brines. Originally we used an Irish soft brine recipe that had sea salt, sugar, curing salt and water in exact proportions. Then, after reading Jane Grigson, I began to put a twist on this classic recipe. In a clean coffee grinder, we blitz down a mixture of peppercorns, rosemary, juniper berries and thyme (you can of course add other ingredients that strike you as suitable, like clove or allspice). We then tie up the mixture in a small square of cheesecloth (if you were to do this at home you can use the type of muslin caps worn by workers in food plants). A litre of the brine is then boiled up and the 'teabag' concoction of spices is added to steep and draw out their flavours. This is then added back into the brine

bath that has by now had the salts all stirred in and settled, and together this makes the matrix of your brine. At this point I add a bottle of white wine as well. So, you can say I have brought in a bit of the European and combined it with the logic of the soft Irish brine.

With dry curing, salt takes a week to travel naturally through an inch of meat, so with a massive leg joint an injector is needed to get the brine all the way through to the centre bone. Speed is a factor in the process – the sooner you get to curing after slaughtering the pig, the better, as fresh meat absorbs the cure more quickly.

Following the traditional Irish method of dry curing, called 'hard cure', you take a piece of pork, put it into a barrel and completely cover it with salt. After some time, when you want to eat it, you dig it out, and of course it has gone rock hard and is fiercely salty. This ham would have been steeped and cooked in a certain way. You'd hear of suggestions of boiling the ham, ladling off the foam, then changing the water and boiling it again, taking off more foam, and so on until there was no more foam rising to the surface. Then you'd have the traditional bit of Irish bacon or ham, a wonderful but always salty experience.

One major consideration for curing is the kind of pork you are going to be using. Is it a pig from a commercial factory system, which has been reared in a warm environment and slaughtered younger so that the meat is softer and wetter, or is it a pig which has been less intensively reared producing meat that is firmer and more dense? A less intensively reared pig, being more slowly grown, will have harder fat due to, amongst other things, cold nights, and the fat is where the flavour is. The softer, wetter meat absorbs salt in a different way too, much faster than slowly raised animals, so that if you were to put these two into exactly the same amount of salt you'd find the commercial pork would be saltier. It's like comparing a pine tree and an oak!

The ultimate pork is, of course, from free-range and outdoor-reared pigs: the difference between the two in short is that a free-range pig has been born and reared entirely in the field, outdoor reared pigs may have been born inside and then moved to fields or be from sheds with outdoor access.

When I started to develop my range I was looking for a traditional dry-cured rasher like the ones I used to taste out at Chris Jepson's smokehouse, where loins of bacon dusted in pepper hung from the ceiling. These he cured just like his salmon, using what is called the dredging principle: you fill a deep tray with salt and, if you want, sugars, herbs and spices. Then you take your piece of meat and roll it around in the mix. (The amount that sticks to the surface is the amount you will need.) You let the meat lie in this for about four days, occasionally turning it.

We work our bacon in an alternative way. We weigh each belly or loin, calculating for about 30g of our cure to each kilo of meat. We rub as much of this mix as we can on both sides before they are laid down in tubs, all tightly packed with no air between. The tubs are filled right to the top, closed tightly, then stored in our coldrooms. During the process we will flip over the pieces a couple of times and massage them until the salt has penetrated. Then they are taken out of the tubs. Remembering that it takes a week for salt to penetrate through an inch of meat, you have to allow for each loin or belly, which can vary from bellies of 1–2 inches up to loins of 3–4 inches. Note that the salt is penetrating from both sides of the salted surfaces to meet in the middle. After the two-week period they are washed and put up on hooks to dry.

If the right pig comes along, one with a big fatty belly, this we will separate to make pancetta.

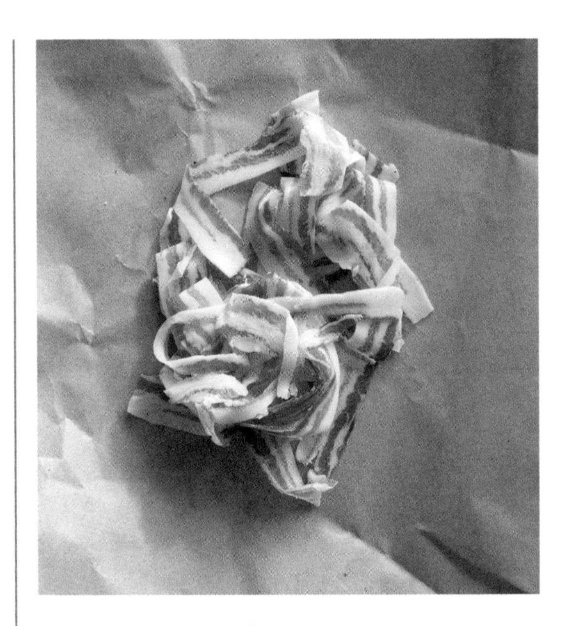

It's just like making streaky bacon, but we add 35g of dry-cure blend per kg of belly, rubbing it in fully, then vacuum-pack it and leave it for two weeks, turning and massaging periodically. At the end of the fortnight we wash off all the cure, hang it in the smoker for a day, then in the salami maturation room where we leave it for a minimum of one month.

Dry-cure Blend

(For a 1kg batch of cure)
800g salt
200g sugar
5g juniper berries
2.5g peppercorns
2g dried rosemary
1.5g dried thyme
1g dried bay leaf

In summary, the biggest difference between brining and dry curing is that, at the end of the process, ham in brine will have kept its weight and may even have gained a little as it will have absorbed some of the pickle, making for a juicier, moist cut when boiled, whereas dry-cured bacon will be lighter in weight as the salt will have drawn out the juices from the meat by osmosis, giving you a firmer cut for great sliced rashers and full-flavoured roast bacon.

Smoking

We use two types of wood for smoking: oak and beech. We are blessed with friends and family locally who have big trees that come down in the wind and find their way to us. These we cut into large rings with a chainsaw, then split them into generous-sized logs with an axe (as Tom would say, 'A man who cuts wood warms himself twice') and pile them in the shed to dry. The ideal wood is a good dried heartwood – you don't want to use green wood for a smoker, as the high moisture content prevents it from burning properly. We avoid too much bark or spalted (discoloured by fungus) wood as well. We look for quality wood that burns evenly with good heat and creates a good smoke.

The principle of our smoker is similar to that of making charcoal: the gentle smouldering-down of the wood, with no flame involved, burns it right the way through. The kiln we use is the size of a beer keg, with a raised fire grate at the base. Beneath the grate is an adjustable air vent that allows a controlled amount of air into the smoker: fully opened for lighting and half-closed when smoking. The lid is adjustable as well, for added control over the amount of smoke that leaves the kiln during the smoking process. The reason that the balance between the air in and the smoke out is so important is that a smoker with insufficient air coming in gives off a bitter smoke, and one with too much air in it just burns off too quickly, with low smoke output.

This kiln is a refinement on a traditional pit smoker, where you would light a fire in the ground and pipe the smoke up into your smokehouse. Ours can be lit outside in the fresh air, simply by sticking a blowtorch into the base of the kiln: after 10 minutes a roaring fire is established. The lid is then replaced, snuffing out the fire and half-closing the bottom flap. This at first throws a harsh, hacking, black smoke which, after the air input it is balanced by use of the lid and the bottom flap, turns into a subtle, perfumed, whisping, white smoke that means we can now wheel the kiln into our smokehouse. One generous armful of wood will smoulder for up to eight hours.

We have two of these smokers on our farm. The first is for cheese smoking, in the dairy, where it is housed in its own dedicated room away from the cheesemaking. Again, we're looking here for quality smoke rather than heat. So I designed it to have a low pit where we light the smoker, from which a metal hood funnels the smoke through a narrow slit into the neighbouring smoke chamber containing the cheeses. This room has a false floor with holes bored into it – more at the back than the front – allowing the smoke to travel evenly up through the floor and fill the chamber. We believe less is more, and to achieve a subtle smoked cheese we use an undertone of quality smoke over the course of four days.

Down in the Smokehouse, we use the same basic principle with our second smoker, but here we place the kiln in the centre of the smoke

chamber with all the meats we want to smoke hanging from sticks high in the roof. We like a little bit of heat in this chamber as it encourages more colour and penetration of flavour into the meats, but we never allow the temperature to go above 40°C. Here we smoke our hams, salamis and bacon. Smouldering down the sweet hardwoods definitely gives us a unique, defined signature flavour and aroma, which you notice as soon as you walk into the building.

Several years ago I developed a project to build a Texan pit smoker. I asked my friend J. J. Bowen at the local forge to help me build a giant mobile barbecue. This monster, constructed of quarter-inch steel to retain heat with two strong axles under it, weighs over a tonne. It's painted jet black and the main door, which lifts up to reveal the cooking chamber, has a large counter-balance. It is an amalgamation of a wood-fired oven with a fire box at the tail end, lower than the cooking chamber, in which you light a fire from good-quality dense hardwoods for a hot, smokeless heat.

The cooking chamber, which makes up the main barrel of the smoker, can hold a whole pig or can be adapted to hold three or four box-meshed shelves that can be loaded with various cuts or dishes. As in the meat smoker in the Smokehouse, the same principle of balancing the air in and the smoke out applies, and there are various levers and flaps to control this process, similar in many ways to (and inspired by) the original smoker. It cooks at 100°C – low and slow. This style was originally designed for Texan foods such as brisket, ribs and pulled pork. All of these meats would be prepared with a 'rub', which is a combination of salt, sugars, herbs and spices. Slow cooking with smoke seals the meat and forms what in the barbecue world is called a 'bark' – combine this with a mopping sauce and marinades and you've got the perfect set-up to feed big numbers at festivals, weddings and parties.

Future Plans

The smokehouse started off as a hobby – we had the pigs in our fields, their pork in our freezers, and a smoker with two chambers: one for the cheese and another that was crying out to be used.

We went from my having two pigs to the scale we are now, where there are six other people helping me in the Smokehouse to produce our range of meats. It feels like we are now reaching the start of the next phase – pulling all of the operational elements of Gubbeen together, allowing the Smokehouse to grow while staying true to the quality of what we are producing.

The availability of non-intensively reared pork has long been a problem for food producers who are operating to scales larger than those of a smallholder. Our compromise at present involves the use of some locally sourced, commercially reared Irish pork to fill the gap. A number of years ago we started buying pork from small, independent, local farmers – the start of what I call our Pig-Co-Op. The Pig-Co-Op would move us to a point where all of the pork used in our growing Smokehouse comes from our own farm at Gubbeen and from other local farms. Our hope is that we can ensure that the rearing of our pigs is not rushed, that they are fed natural feeds from local mills designed to give the best nutritional results, and that we can continue to use a mix of traditional breeds. This will give the Smokehouse a steady, reliable supply of the very best quality ingredients while sustaining local growth and regeneration.

Our community is also important to me – as a small food producer there is a strong sense of being a part of a bigger family. Our friends and the connections we've made in this business keep us passionate about what we do. I get drawn in by customers' enthusiasm for something different and by their excitement about certain products. It makes me want to keep developing and experimenting, to come up with something new and wonderful for them.

I want these connections to stay an integral part of Gubbeen and to remain a part of the future for my children. I would be proud to think that what we do now will become a part of what they can take on for their future at Gubbeen. Food production, the farm itself and the care of the land – these are things that I always bear in mind.

Chorizo

This is one of the greats – a good chorizo will make any dish take heart. I tasted chorizo first when I was tiny, with my Spanish family in Andalucía – it was one of the reasons I became a charcutier!
Notes on ingredients:
** As we sell into commercial markets we use curing salts that contain nitrites, which play a large part in food safety and shelf life, though they are not essential if making salami just for yourself.*
** Sodium nitrate/potassium nitrate need very careful measurement, preferably added via a curing salt mix (there are ready-mixed products you can buy, such as 'pink salt' or Prague Powder, in which the nitrite is evenly distributed through plain salt). If you can find curing salts on a butcher supply website you need to add 2g per kilo of pork to the spice mix.*

EQUIPMENT
Mincer
Sausage filler
Butcher's twine

MAKES 3 × 18CM LONG CHORIZOS OF 45–50MM DIAMETER (WHICH WILL SHRINK DOWN AS THEY MATURE)

I recommend making your chorizo in batches of at least 5kg. Of course you will need to multiply all the ingredients accordingly.

1kg pork, ideally with a meat-to-fat ratio of 3:1 – ask your butcher to mince very coarsely or, if you can mince, use a 8mm plate or bigger

Fermentation
For our salamis and chorizo we count on a fermentation process for the development of those unique salami flavours. To encourage and control this process we add lactic cultures which, like cheese cultures, produce acidity as they multiply, feeding on available sugars. For us this gives us consistency. When I started I never bought these and counted on the natural presence in the environment – but I must admit this did give me an inconsistent result.

Different strains of cultures may be used for different results, such as changes in acidity levels or speed of fermentation, so you must follow the supplier's instructions and advice carefully.

The dextrose we use is a simple sugar (as opposed to a complex sugar like table sugars), an instantly digestible, convertible one for the cultures to feed on. Again, like the lactic cultures, this is to maintain the desired results but is not essential as there are natural sugars present in the meat.

Mix the cultures in a cupful of chlorine-free water at body temperature and allow them time to wake up from their frozen state. Add this solution to the meat 1 hour before adding any salt and spice blend, as salt will inhibit the cultures multiplying.

Mixing and Mincing
Combine all of the remaining flavouring ingredients with your minced meat. Vigorously mix everything together until the meat starts to feel tacky and sticky, making sure to keep the meat below 6°C.

Pinch of culture, or follow instructions from supplier
19g salt
2g curing salt
6g dextrose
10g sweet paprika
10g hot paprika
1g ground black pepper
0.5g dried oregano
6g fresh garlic
0.5g chilli pepper flakes
1 tablespoon golden syrup (optional)*

For the Casings

1 hank 45–50mm diameter salted natural beef casings
1 lemon
1 teaspoon bicarbonate of soda

Casings come in bundles called hanks. You might need to buy one whole hank, which will make up to 8kg chorizo – you can re-salt surplus casing for storage for another day.

*Golden syrup is a complex sugar and so doesn't affect fermentation. I use it to marry the smoked flavour with the heat of the spices.

After mixing in the spices, take about one third of the meat mixture and now mince this again through a finer plate, a 3.5mm. This finer mince will act as a binder for the coarser meat, which you will now mix it with.

To marinate this mixture, pat it down firmly into a plastic container, cover and chill it overnight.

Preparing and Filling the Casings

Wash all salt off the casings and leave in a bucket of cold water overnight with a piece of crushed lemon – a natural antiseptic that will keep them fresh.

Rinse your casings by running about a cup of cold water into the open end, then working it through to the other end. This will also loosen them, gently removing tangles and knots.

Leave the casings in a bowl filled with tepid water with the open end hanging over the side. Add the bicarbonate of soda to the water. This will make the casings soft and slippery, which will help when running them onto your stuffing nozzle.

Insert the meat mixture into a sausage filler a bit at a time, packing it down to prevent any air bubbles in the mix, and attach the first casing to the stuffing nozzle.

Once the casings are filled to your desired length, tie off the ends with a butterfly knot (like a double reef knot, the second knot pinching the casing to prevent the knots from slipping). Weigh them now and make a note of the fresh weight on a label for each sausage.

To remove any air bubbles, stab the casings with a pin multiple times, then hang the chorizo on hooks or over sticks to dry. (I make hooks from fencing wire, which can be bent by hand.)

Incubation and Drying

Hang your casings somewhere warm to drip dry – ideally you want the chorizo to warm up slowly to 27°C in a humid place so the casings don't harden. A damp warm atmosphere will accelerate fermentation. After 24 hours they are ready to be smoked (see page 151).

Hang them next in an airy place like a pantry where conditions are as near as possible to 75 per cent humidity and 15°C. If moulds appear on the surface of your chorizo, wipe them off with diluted cooking alcohol like brandy or vodka which will sterilise the casings. Alternatively, you can re-smoke them.

When they have lost a third of their weight, they are ready to try!

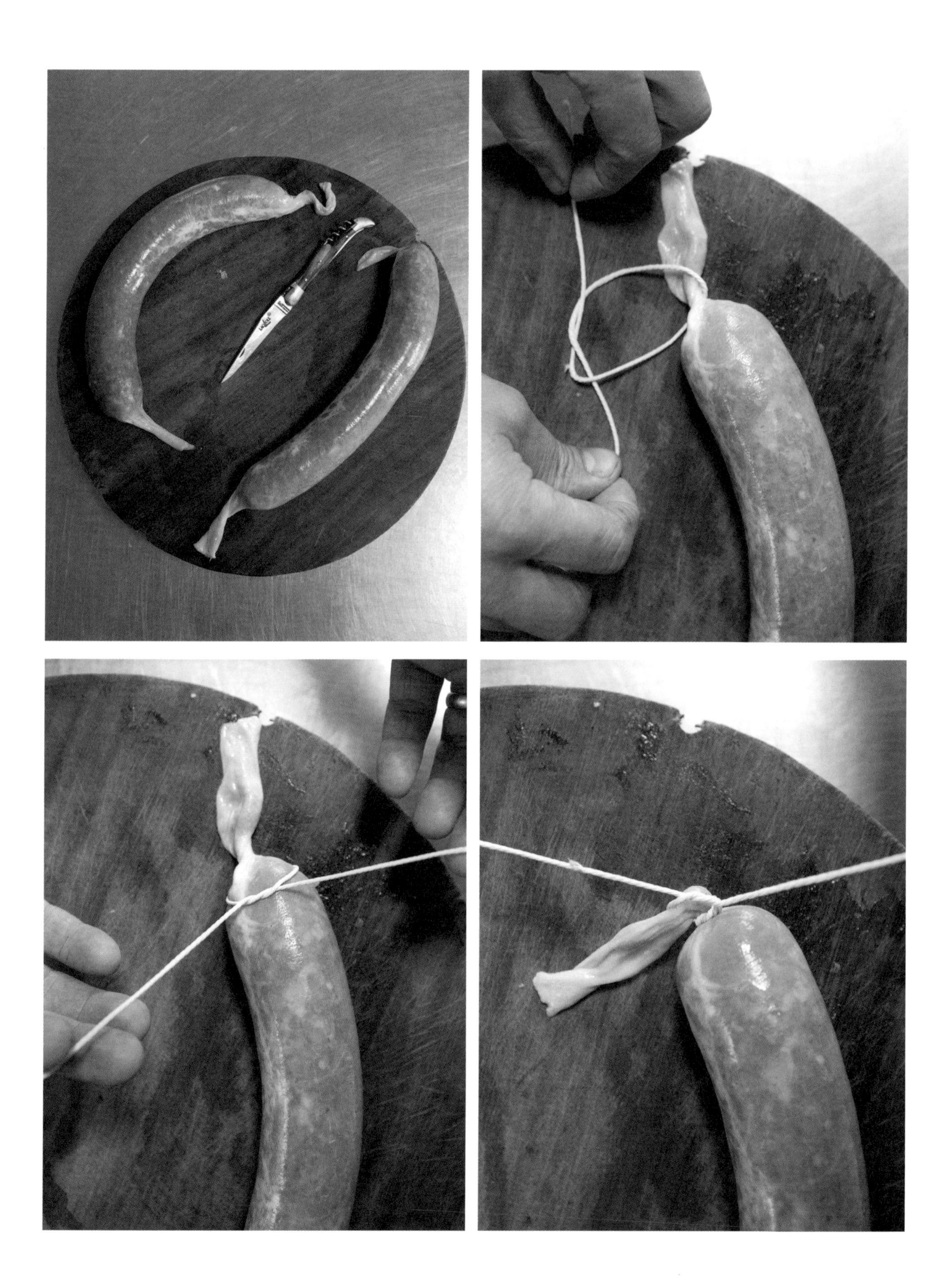

Pepperoni

I really got to know the true pepperoni on trips to the Salone del Gusto in Turin – I believe the origin of the name is the little hot peppers of southern Italy called peperone. *We use chilli pepper flakes, and I also add garlic powder as I like a dry mixture for these little sausages.*

Our Irish offerings are perhaps a little softer and slightly less hot than the original, but as I have children eating these now we do seem to have cracked it; I am really proud when I see these young customers come to our market stall with their pocket money, keen to buy these instead of sweets!

EQUIPMENT
Mincer
Sausage filler

MAKES ABOUT 6 × 25CM LONG PEPPERONIS

1kg pork – shoulder is perfect, 80 per cent lean and 20 per cent fat
18g salt
1g ground coriander
1g ground fennel seeds
0.5g garlic powder
0.5g chilli pepper flakes
6.25g dextrose
20g golden syrup
Small pinch of culture – follow supplier's instructions
20mm collagen casings – source from a good but alternative butcher or butcher supply store

Mincing and Mixing
While working with meat, do keep your mix as cold as possible – under 6°C.

Coarsely mince the pork using either the biggest mincing plate or the grinder attachment on your mincer, KitchenAid or Kenwood are both good: it will have roughly 8–10mm holes. Add in all the flavouring ingredients and mix well.

Now finely mince the pork again (use a plate with 2–3mm holes) and mix vigorously until the meat starts to feel sticky and tacky.

Pack the mixture into a tub and chill it down in the fridge overnight to start the culture development.

Filling
The following day, transfer the finely minced sausage mixture to your sausage filler, in batches if necessary, depending on the size of your machine. Pack it down to prevent any air bubbles in the mix, and attach the first casing to the stuffing nozzle. Attach a soaked casing to your sausage filler or attachment and gently fill, but not too tightly.

With long casings, twist them roughly every 25cm to make separate pepperoni, and use a pin to prick any air bubbles.

Incubation and Drying
Hang your pepperoni draped over a stick (I use broom handles or wooden dowel) somewhere warm – ideally you want the pepperoni to warm up slowly to 27°C in a humid place. A damp warm atmosphere will accelerate fermentation. After 24 hours they are ready to be smoked (see page 151).

After smoking, you can now move them somewhere to dry in a cool (15°C is perfect), airy, clean space – the old pantry of country houses is the model. After they have lost a third of their weight they should be ready to eat.

Sausages

There is a huge range of sausages available in shops but few that have a high meat content, are gluten-free and contain no chemicals or artificial preservatives. Making your own sausages allows you to control the quality of the meat and ingredients – it's also a lot of fun for a like-minded group of friends or family to do together.

When making sausages it is important that you get good-quality meat from your butcher. I recommend a meat-to-fat ratio of 3:1 or 4:1 depending on the style of sausage. Ask your butcher for pork belly if you're using pork. Say that it is being used for sausage making and could they help you out – you need to avoid any gristle, skin or sinew which will come though in the end result. A good master butcher, or a butcher's supply store website, is where you may be able to get your sausage casing too. My preference is to use natural sheep casings; collagen casings are also very good for homemade sausages and they don't need soaking.

MAKES 34 SAUSAGES OF 26MM DIAMETER

EQUIPMENT
Mincer
Sausage filler

Sun-dried Tomato, Garlic and Basil Sausage
2kg pork, diced
100g sun-dried tomatoes – dry form, not oiled
30g fresh or frozen basil
7g garlic, finely chopped
20g sea salt
10g raw cane sugar

Fresh Italian Sausage
2kg pork, diced
24g sea salt
15g raw cane sugar
8g garlic, finely chopped
6g ground black pepper
5g ground fennel seeds
2g chilli pepper flakes
1g ground cumin

Start the process by mincing the meat coarsely. Use either the biggest mincing plate or the grinder attachment on your mincer, KitchenAid or Kenwood are best: it will have holes roughly 8–10mm. If you do not have one of these gadgets, simply chop the meat into small pieces.

Put the meat on a tray and chill for 1 hour. This will help keep the temperature down during the make. (Chilling the meat as much as you can is important because this ensures you get a good emulsion or texture in the sausage meat; it also helps with the shelf life and storage time for the sausage. I suggest putting it in the freezer, because usually a regular household fridge is set between 3 and 5°C, which is not cold enough.)

Now for the second mincing. Take the chilled meat mixture and put it through a finer mincing plate with holes of 2–3mm diameter. A trick to chill the meat as cold as 4°C for this second mincing is to add a small amount of crushed ice to it while mincing. If you want a fine-textured sausage, you could use your food processor blade and bowl (but avoid over-mincing and don't allow it to warm to above 6°C).

After this second mincing give the meat a further mixing by hand and tightly pack it into a tub or bowl. Refrigerate until your are ready to make your sausages.

Tip: If you don't own a mincer, you can always buy finely minced pork, add your flavouring ingredients to this meat and mix by hand until the mixture gets sticky on your hands – but still avoid the meat getting too warm!

Merguez Sausages

- 2kg lamb or mutton (if the lamb is very lean, add some pork fat)
- 60g harissa paste
- 20g sea salt
- 20g paprika
- 12g garlic
- 10g raw cane sugar
- 6g ground black pepper
- 3g ground fennel seeds
- 1g ground cinnamon
- 1g cayenne pepper (optional)

Choose your desired diameter size for the sausages – I like to use 26–28mm casings – and prepare them as described on page 157.

Transfer the finely minced sausage mixture to your sausage filler, in batches if necessary, depending on the size of your machine. Pack it down to prevent any air bubbles in the mix, and attach the first casing to the stuffing nozzle.

When you fill the casings, avoid over-filling, otherwise the sausages will burst when you start to twist them off. It may take a couple of goes, but the slower you work, the easier it is. With a long casing, twist roughly every 15cm to make separate sausage links, and use a pin to prick any air bubbles.

Refrigerate or freeze the sausages in batches. These will now store in the fridge for about 3 days.

Tuscan Soppressata
(Pig's Head 'Cheese')

The beauty of this dish is that you don't have to worry about getting brines right as you would with the French or English brawns. Once the head is boiled and the meat pulled away, the fun of the flavouring is in your hands, and you can be creative. We really love it with pickles – especially little dill pickles and the balsamic sweet pickled onions.

MAKES 1KG

EQUIPMENT
Large square of clean cheesecloth

1 clean, shaved pig's head, split in half, ears removed
1 cinnamon stick
6 cloves
12 black peppercorns
About 2.5 litres ham or chicken stock
½ teaspoon ground cinnamon
Pinch of ground cloves
Maldon-style sea salt
Freshly ground black pepper

Preheat the oven to 150°C/gas mark 2.

Place the head and ears in a very large pot of water, bring to the boil and boil for 5 minutes. Drain the water. The pot will be hot and heavy, so do be careful. Rinse the head and ears in a colander with clean water.

You might have to wash up the pot you just boiled the head in if that's the only one you own big enough to house it comfortably; it needs to be an ovenproof pot.

So, back into the pot go your pig's head and ears along with the cinnamon stick, cloves and peppercorns. Add the stock until the meat is just covered, and taste for seasoning. Depending on the shape and size of your pot, you may need to top up the stock level. If you don't have quite enough stock, top up with some white wine, cider or, last resort, water.

Cover with greaseproof paper and weigh the head down with an ovenproof plate so that it is fully submerged. Seal with tinfoil or a lid and braise in the oven for 2½ hours. The meat should part easily from the bone when you check it. Needless to say, continue cooking until it does.

Remove the braised pig's head from the oven and allow it cool down in the stock. You can accelerate the cooling process by placing the pot in a sinkful of iced or very cold water. (If you take the head out while it is hot, the skin toughens and becomes inedible.)

Once the head and ears are cool enough to handle, start separating the meat from the bone. A large tray will come in handy here. After the bone has been removed examine the meat and remove anything that looks like it wouldn't be pleasant to eat, such as the glands in the jowl and the cartilage near the tip of the snout. Keep an eye out for any rogue peppercorns or cloves. Strain the stock, cool further and refrigerate.

Transfer half the head meat to a chopping board and dice into chunks or pull apart with your hands and place in a bowl. You don't have to be too fancy about this. Repeat with the other half. Slice the ears matchstick thin and mix with the head meat. Season well with Maldon salt, a grind of pepper and the ground cinnamon. Taste as you go: if you feel the meat needs a little more of any of these seasonings; add it pinch by pinch. Lastly add the ground cloves. Don't mix too vigorously: you don't want to mash the meat as this will affect the future texture of your 'head cheese'.

Tip all the meat mix into the centre of a clean square of cheesecloth. Arrange the meat into a roll and bring the cloth up and over much like a Christmas cracker. It needs to be packed tightly in the roll. Once it is firm, tie up the ends and reinforce with string – you should end up with something resembling a large salami.

Place this big sausage on a tray. Put a chopping board on top and weigh this down with something heavy like a house brick to 'press' the roll. Make sure it's well balanced. If possible, place this whole arrangement overnight in a cold room or in the bottom of your fridge. You could also place it in an icebox with ice packs to cool it all down – ensure the ice is in a watertight bag if you're following this method. The next day the natural gelatine will have set and you can unroll the now-set pâté.

There: you have your Tuscan Soppressata. Cut into thin slices and serve with cornichons, pickles and crusty bread.

Roast Garlic and Chorizo Soup

This is a soup recipe that came from our good friend Mark Murphy. It is warming and restores faith in life on a cold day.

SERVES 6

- 6 whole garlic bulbs, cloves separated but not peeled
- 4 tablespoons olive oil
- 1 large onion, finely diced
- 2 celery sticks, finely diced
- Small bunch of thyme, leaves picked
- 250g fresh Gubbeen chorizo, cut into small pieces
- ½ teaspoon sweet smoked paprika
- 1.5 litres chicken stock
- Bunch of flat-leaf parsley, leaves stripped and finely chopped, to serve
- Salt and freshly ground black pepper

Preheat the oven to 180°C/gas mark 4.

Put the garlic cloves in a baking tray with 2 tablespoons of the oil, cover with tinfoil and cook in the oven for about 25–30 minutes. At this point the cloves should be golden and soft. Allow them to cool slightly and reserve the oil. When the garlic is cool enough to handle, peel it and blend it to a purée.

Heat the rest of the oil in a large heavy-bottomed pot over a medium heat, then add the diced onion plus a pinch of salt. Cook gently for about 5 minutes, add the celery and thyme leaves and continue to cook for a further 5 minutes.

Turn up the heat slightly, add the chorizo and cook for about 3 minutes or until the chorizo has caramelised slightly. Stir in the smoked paprika and mix well. Add the roasted garlic purée and the chicken stock to the pot. Bring to a simmer and leave it to simmer for about 15 minutes. Taste and season with salt and black pepper.

To serve, add the chopped parsley and drizzle some of the reserved oil from the roasted garlic on top.

Bean and Sausage Stew

Yes, you are right, this is a take on cassoulet. It was one of the great family dishes all through the hungry years when you couldn't fill the children up enough. It is famously better on day 2, and could always be made and kept in the fridge for a day with the crumb added separately.

SERVES 2 ADULTS AND 3 CHILDREN

14 sausages, such as a Sun-dried Tomato, Garlic and Basil or Fresh Italian (see page 162)

For the beans
300g butter beans
1 tablespoon mild olive oil
1 large carrot, cut into 5 or 6 chunks
1 large onion, cut into 6
½ leek, cut into large rounds
1 sprig of rosemary
1 sprig of thyme
Salt

For the crumb
½ loaf or 400g of stale bread or Malthouse Sourdough (see page 232)
2 tablespoons mild olive oil

For the stew base
50g butter
4 medium onions, thinly sliced
6 garlic cloves
1 sprig of thyme
1 tablespoon white wine vinegar
1 chilli, seeds removed, finely diced (try a mild red)
2 tablespoons Dijon mustard

Soak the butter beans in cold water overnight or for at least 4 hours.

When you are ready to cook, preheat the oven to 180°C/gas mark 4.

Tip the beans into a colander and rinse, then set aside to drain.

To cook the beans, set a pot over a medium heat and add the olive oil. Fry the carrot, onion and leek until lightly coloured. Add the rosemary, thyme and the beans and cover with about 4cm water. Bring everything to the boil, then simmer for about 20 minutes until the beans are cooked but retain a little bite. Season this stock water, discard the vegetables and herbs, and allow the beans to cool in the liquid ready for use or refrigerate until needed.

Remove the crust from the bread and discard. Rub the bread between your fingers to form crumbs.

While the beans are cooking, start the base for the stew. Melt the butter in a pot with a lid, add the onions, garlic, a pinch of salt and the thyme, and cook until the onions are soft and sweet. Add the vinegar and the chilli. Cook for a further 5 minutes then mix in the mustard and the beans. Check the seasoning and adjust to taste.

Brown the sausages in a frying pan, shaking the pan so that they colour evenly, and add them to the stew base.

Transfer everything except the breadcrumbs into a sizeable ovenproof casserole dish and put in the oven for 15–20 minutes. While the stew cooks, mix the olive oil into the breadcrumbs, a drizzle at a time, until they are just about coated. Remove the stew from the oven, cover liberally with the breadcrumbs and bake for a further 15 minutes until the surface crumbs are toasted.

Serve with lots of steamed greens or roasted parsnips. Mustard should always be to hand when eating this dish.

Pulled Pork with Celeriac Remoulade Sandwich

Pulled pork has been reinvented by the great southern states of America's barbecue styles. It is the very essence of comfort food. It is certainly a dish that needs lots of premeditation as it cooks so slowly, but once it is there for you everything works: it is tender, juicy and all the accompaniments are just delicious.

MAKES **12–15** LARGE SANDWICHES
(leftover cooked pork can be wrapped and frozen for future sandwiches)

1 shoulder of pork, hand removed, well hung, skin scored

For the remoulade
1 head of celeriac
3 tablespoons Dijon mustard
1 tablespoon crème fraîche
2 tablespoons superfine capers or chopped capers
100g flat-leaf or curly parsley, roughly chopped
2 x 47.5g tins best-quality anchovies, drained and roughly chopped (Ortiz are perfect, but if you can't get exceptional anchovies, omit them)
Squeeze of lemon juice
1 glass of cider (optional)
Salt and freshly ground black pepper

1 loaf of Malthouse Sourdough (see page 232), to serve

Preheat the oven to 90°C/gas mark ¼ .

Heavily salt the shoulder of pork all over. Place it on a rack in a baking tray and slow roast in the oven. Depending on the size of the shoulder this can take anywhere between 8 and 10 hours to get to the point where the meat will tear or 'pull'. If you wish to eat this in the afternoon, it's a good idea to put the shoulder in the oven the night before. It is cooked so low that the shoulder never gets stressed – the meat must have totally surrendered before you remove it from the oven. Take the shoulder out of the oven and allow to cool on the rack in the tray: this will catch all the juices and fat that will seep out. Keep everything in the tray – you'll need it later.

When the shoulder is just finishing in the oven or cooling is the perfect time to make the remoulade. Peel the celeriac, cut into manageable chunks and thinly slice with a sharp knife. You should end up with large 'petals' of thin celeriac. Stack the slices 4 or 5 high and cut into thin matchsticks.

Combine the mustard, crème fraîche, capers and parsley in a large bowl and add the celeriac matchsticks. Mix together well and fold in the anchovies with care so the delicate flesh isn't damaged too much. Adjust the acidity with the lemon juice to taste. Leave at room temperature if you intend to pull the pork and make the sandwich, or cover and refrigerate if you are organised and getting ahead.

When the shoulder is cool enough to handle, you can start to pull the pork. Needless to say, very clean hands are imperative; gloves are very handy. Remove the skin (sadly the skin needs to be sacrificed in order to get fantastic pulled pork) and shred the meat into a large bowl. When all the meat is picked, add the fat and the juices from the roasting tray and mix gently. Taste the meat and add salt and pepper until you're happy with the seasoning. A glass of cider lifts the mix but it's not imperative.

Slice the whole sourdough and use to make sandwiches filled with as much pulled pork as you dare, followed by a layer of the celeriac remoulade.

Ham Hock and Lentils

I was about 16 when I first went to Spain to live for a year with my family. My father was a writer and a romantic – sun, olive oil, lemons and wine made a small farm in Andalucía a joy that never lost its power for him. All my Spanish family are wonderful cooks and all talk about food and generally celebrate it in every way; when I miss them badly on wet, cold Irish winter evenings there is always food therapy, Sopa de Lentejas *being the best cure. What brings back the old kitchen in La Almona, the fun I had with my wonderful brothers and sisters, is the smell of a garlic bulb turned on the hot ring of the Aga until it browns and scalds a little; the Aga ring works just like the* plancha *– a metal griddle plate that you will find in every Andaluz kitchen. The garlic is thrown into the pot and does powerful things to this wonderful soup. Even if I slightly change the recipe every time I make it, the charred garlic is always included.*

My family all lived in Ireland and went to school here, so their food-therapy support in midsummer, when they are wilting with the heat, is a cup of Barry's Tea!

SERVES 6

1 smoked ham hock
1 green ham hock
1 large onion, roughly chopped
1 carrot, roughly chopped
Small bunch of thyme
250g Puy lentils
2 leeks, sliced into 1cm rounds
6 garlic cloves, sliced
60g butter
2 tablespoons Dijon mustard
1 glass of red wine (optional)
Handful of cornichons, roughly chopped
Salt
6 fistfuls of spinach or other leafy green vegetable, to serve

Preheat the oven to 130°C/gas mark 1. Put the ham hocks into a pot that accommodates them comfortably, cover with water and bring to a swift boil. Discard the water and rinse away any scum that might be clinging to the hocks. You might have to wash your pot at this point.

Put the ham hocks back in the pot (make sure it's ovenproof if you are going to be braising in the oven), cover with water again and add the onion, carrot and thyme. Bring back up to the boil, then immediately turn down to a simmer. Cook in the oven for about 2 hours; alternatively simmer gently on the hob. (The hams are ready when the small bone at the thinner end pops out easily.) If you take the hocks out of the liquor when they're just done they will steam and dry out, so leave them to rest in the liquid once out of the oven or off the heat.

While the hams are resting, start to cook the lentils. Put them in a pan and just cover them with water. Boil them for 5 minutes, strain off the water through a sieve and rinse under cold water.

Return the pan you used to cook the lentils to the heat and fry the leeks and garlic in the butter until soft and translucent, then add the lentils back to the pan. Ladle enough of the ham liquor into the pan to cover the lentils by about 3cm. Bring them to the boil, then simmer for about 20 minutes until tender but still with a little bite to them. Season to taste and add red wine if you like. As the ham stock should be fairly well seasoned, you may only require a pinch of salt.

When you're ready to serve, stir the Dijon mustard into the lentils. Add more or less, depending on how you like it. Wilt your chosen leaf, stir the cornichons into the lentils, then spoon everything into your serving dish. Place the hocks in top.

Marinade for Ribs or Pork Chops

Cooking meat using a pit smoker or slowly on a barbecue requires good marinades and mops (I thin out some marinade with beer to 'mop' the meat with) to boost the flavour and prevent the meat from drying out while creating a gorgeous sticky crust.

To prepare the ribs you need to take a rack of ribs or loin ribs and remove the membrane from the non-meaty side. Using a clean dishcloth to get a better grip of the membrane, scratch it from the cut end of the rib edge and pull this membrane away from the ribs – nine times out of ten it will come away in a single pull.

I have several recipes for marinades that I play with, but this is my favourite.

MAKES ABOUT 1 LITRE
enough for an entire rack of ribs and more

500ml homemade or store-bought simple BBQ sauce
250ml olive oil
2 large tablespoons sweet paprika
2 large tablespoons harissa (North African hot chilli paste)
1 large tablespoon ground black pepper
1 large tablespoon lemon juice
½ teaspoon rosemary
¼ teaspoon thyme
¼ teaspoon ground cumin
¼ teaspoon garlic powder

Mix together the marinade ingredients and smear all over both sides of the ribs. Cover with clingfilm and refrigerate for at least a few hours – overnight if possible. It is good to keep back a little of the marinade so that you can baste the meat during cooking. There are three ways you could cook the ribs:

Oven
Preheat the oven to 130°C/gas mark 1. Place the ribs on a baking tray and cover with tinfoil. Bake in the oven for 4 hours, basting the ribs with some of the remaining marinade every hour, as required, until the meat is tender and falling off the bones.

Hot Smoker
Preheat the hot smoker to 100°C with a mild smoke – I use oak shavings but any good hardwood like ash, beech or apple will work. Place the marinated ribs on the smoking rack for 3 hours. Remove the ribs, wrap them in butcher's paper or tinfoil and return to the smoker for a further 2 hours.

When you remove the ribs from the wrapping you will notice that they have shrunk back on the bone, giving almost a French-trim appearance. This means they are ready to eat and the meat should literally fall off the bone. If you want you could give the unwrapped ribs a quick mopping with barbecue sauce and cook for a further hour – the result is a divine, smoky-sweet flavour.

Barbecue
If cooking on a barbecue with a lid, place the ribs on the opposite side of the barbecue from the heat source, be it gas or (my preference) charcoal. This prevents the meat getting burnt, but gives the flavours of a barbecue while cooking more like an oven. What is also nice about charcoal is that it starts off with a higher heat that wanes during the cooking process, allowing for a longer cooking time and therefore more tender ribs. If cooking on an open barbecue I recommend pre-cooking the ribs in an oven and finishing on the barbecue for the chargrill flavour.

Ham, Gubbeen and Pickled Chicory

This is a recipe that has brought a really exciting and productive collaboration into our life here at Gubbeen. Small food producers will never really reach into the heart of cities without the support and friendship of chefs. Lee Tiernan has offered both these things.

Up until recently Lee was head chef at St John Bread & Wine in London. One day Lee had a batch of slightly overcooked ox tongues and had to turn them into hash. Provided with the perfect excuse to find a good melting cheese for the top of his hash, he visited a cheese shop and bought four different cheeses to see which one melted best. It was Gubbeen that won out for him. Lee made Gubbeen Cream for the first time before service (see page 218). Ox Tongue Hash and Gubbeen went on the restaurant menu that evening and sold out. Gubbeen started to turn up everywhere after that: with brisket, ham, smoked haddock and in soups. So our thanks goes to Lee and Fergus Henderson, founder of St John! Pickled chicory is a stock pickle for that great restaurant and has been on their menus since the very beginning.

SERVES 4–6

For the pickled chicory
900ml white wine vinegar
500g white cane sugar
3 star anise
5 black peppercorns
6 heads of chicory, quartered

1kg new potatoes (Pink Fir apple is a favourite)
1 tablespoon salt
2 tablespoons Dijon mustard
Juice of ½ lemon
100ml olive oil
2 spring onions, thinly sliced
1 tablespoon chopped curly parsley
About 250g leftover ham, pulled into nice pieces
250g Gubbeen cheese, thinly sliced
Freshly ground black pepper
150ml Gubbeen Cream (see page 218), to serve

To make the pickle, put everything except the chicory into a heavy pan and slowly bring up to the boil. Meanwhile, place the chicory in a clean container or pack into a couple of sterilised jars. Once the liquid has come to the boil, allow to cool down a bit. Pour the warm liquid over the chicory and allow to cool, then refrigerate for about 8 hours before eating.

Preheat the oven to 200°C/gas mark 6.

Drop the potatoes into a pan of salted water, bring to the boil, then simmer until tender. Test they are ready by sacrificing one and cutting it in half; it should be cooked but not falling apart. Drain and allow to cool slightly.

Put the mustard, lemon juice, olive oil, spring onions and parsley in a large bowl. Mix together well and add the still-warm potatoes and the pieces of ham. Toss everything together until the potatoes and ham are evenly dressed, grind in some pepper and check the seasoning.

Put the dressed mixture of ham and potatoes into an oven-proof dish suitable for serving. Lay the cheese evenly over the top and bake in the oven for about 5 minutes until the cheese is shiny and melted, but not runny and split.

When the dish goes in the oven, gently heat the Gubbeen Cream in a small pan.

To serve, pour the Gubbeen Cream over the top of the hot dish and finish with a few quarters of pickled chicory.

Platter of Grilled Gin-marinated Pork Tenderloin, Merguez Sausages, Courgettes and Blackened Leeks

SERVES 4

1 medium to large pork tenderloin
8 Merguez sausages (see page 163)
2 courgettes, sliced lengthways
4–6 baby leeks or 2–3 large leeks, halved

For the marinade
1 shot of gin
Juice of ½ small lemon
1 teaspoon Chinese five-spice
2 large garlic cloves, crushed
½ teaspoon ground black pepper
1 teaspoon soy sauce
1 tablespoon olive oil
1 teaspoon chopped ginger
1 teaspoon Dijon mustard
1 teaspoon sugar
Chopped fresh chilli, to taste

First blend together all the ingredients for the marinade (or pound in a pestle and mortar) and apply to the pork several hours in advance of cooking or, even better, allow to marinate in the fridge overnight.

When you're ready to cook, heat a griddle pan or fire up the barbecue – you need a high heat. Remove the tenderloin from the marinade and cook until the entire surface is browned with nice chargrill lines and the internal temperature reaches 68°C. Remove and rest for 3–5 minutes. If the tenderloin is large it may start to burn on the surface, in which case remove it from the griddle or barbecue and finish the cooking in a 180°C/gas mark 4 oven until an internal temperature of 68°C is achieved (a temperature probe makes life so much easier). It should be medium rare, which is just a little pink in the centre, fully cooked but still lovely and juicy; 71°C is well done. The temperature will continue to rise a degree or two during resting. Overcooked pork will be dry and can be disappointing, especially if you have sourced good-quality pork.

Once it has rested, slice the pork into generously thick slices and keep warm.

The Merguez sausages can be cooked in exactly the same manner alongside the pork tenderloin. Turn frequently on the griddle or barbecue to ensure they do not burn.

Once the sausages are cooked, remove from the heat and rest in a warm place while you cook the courgettes and leeks.

Brush the courgette slices and leeks lightly with olive oil and place onto the griddle. Refrain from moving the vegetables too much so that they can get a nice black griddle mark; turn them over once this mark is formed. The courgettes will take less time than the leeks. Remove from the heat and keep warm until ready to serve.

On a nice big warm platter arrange the slices of pork tenderloin, Merguez sausages and the grilled vegetables. Pour any juices from the rested pork over the meat and serve.

Knives

Knives have always been a strong interest for me. My fascination was originally sparked by a knife collection that I inherited from my uncle Harry, Giana's brother. These knives were given to me at a very young age and I don't think I took very good care of them, throwing them at planks of wood and that sort of thing. I didn't at that point appreciate where they came from and the amount of craftsmanship that had gone into them. They were a mixture of flick knives and homemade knives from all over India, also professional French knives manufactured by Sabatier and Laguiole – a wonderful collection of unique objects from his travels.

Only as I grew older did I realise that I was slowly destroying these fantastic tools, and so I started trying to repair them; this was what made me understand their value and their quality. This was around the same time that I was getting into butchering, which gave me an added incentive to learn about the maintenance and care of knives – I realised, for example, that I was pretty terrible at sharpening a blade! Another piece of study.

I became interested enough to begin looking for a do-it-yourself knife kit, and it was easy enough to find one. Your basic kit offers blades in any number of varieties as well as a piece of wood and a bolster. You assemble the parts and – hey presto! – you have a knife. Then of course you begin to customise it, adjusting the shape and material for the handle, trying out different blades, that sort of thing. Inevitably I was soon hooked. I tend to become a bit obsessive about something once I find I have a knack for it. It was fun to experiment and let myself learn from the early mistakes: a big knife would be refashioned into a shorter one, for example, or a chef's knife would become a Santoku knife.

I've come to realise that this is something that gives me great joy, turning a fascination into producing something, be it bread or beer, salami or cheese; then pawing over the process of learning, understanding, improving and perfecting it.

The one person who more than anyone else helped turn my hobby into a craft was Rory Connor. Rory lives out in Ballylickey, about a half-hour's drive from Gubbeen. I have a huge amount of respect for Rory; for him knife-making is not just a craft or a trade, it's an art, so it's not surprising that he is always busy, and never without a long list of people eager to get one of his knives. One parallel between Rory's work and what we do at Gubbeen is that he also makes everything from scratch. Just as we try to maintain the 'field to fork' principle – the milk from our dairy becoming our cheese, the pigs we rear becoming our salami – so Rory cuts the steel and the blocks of wood that become his knives.

A pivotal moment came when Rory let me make a knife with him in his workshop. We spent half a day on one of his grinders, shaping out the blades, he gave me support with tips and showing me tricks of the trade and by the end of the weekend I had made a fantastic knife. After this time spent with Rory I became determined to make knives and make them well, both for my own use and to give as presents. My love for knifemaking has grown and grown ever since.

Not long after that I went off to Kent in the UK with two friends for another knifemaking weekend. One of these friends was Olivier Beaujouan, from On the Wildside in Castlegregory in Kerry – a fascinating gentleman who comes from multi-generations of charcutiers. Olivier makes pâtés and terrines, which we sell at our farmers' markets. He also pickles seaweeds and harvests oysters and periwinkles, and besides this shares my interest in knifemaking. Also along with us was J. J. Bowen, from Bowen's Forge just ten minutes up the road. J. J. is a skilled and creative blacksmith; in his forge are all these wonderful tools – power hammers, kilns, anvils, tongs – all good for knifemaking!

The person running the weekend was Owen Bush, whose focus is on forging. Forging knives essentially means taking a piece of a specific type of steel that can be hardened, heating it up and beating it with hammers. After we had created the shape we wanted, it was ground down and heat-treated. By the end of the weekend we all had a beautiful blade. I've made this sound like a quick and easy process, but the detail that he went into – the metallurgy, understanding different types of steels, how to treat and harden, style, shape and grind – opened up a new world of opportunities for me.

So now I had learned the two methods for making knives: flat grinding, where you cut out the shape of the knife, grind it down to create the bevels in the blade, then heat treat it; and forging, where you shape a blade with heat and hammers and grind it down afterwards – two different styles of knifemaking, two different skills. Considering my background, I suppose it was inevitable that these influences would lead me to making kitchen knives.

The kinds of knives I make fall into two categories: hidden tang and full tang. After spending time with Rory I started making full-tang knives. The blade of a full-tang knife, which stems from European traditions, extends all the way to the bottom of the handle, where it has the same shape as the scales you attach to the handle. When I make this type of knife I aim to create a strong, confident, solid knife that can take any amount of abuse a chef might put it through. This means focusing on the materials, getting the best kind of steel possible.

I save my more adventurous instincts for the hidden-tang knives. These come from a Japanese tradition, and have a spike of metal that connects the blade into the handle. The handles in this style can be carved into any shape I choose. This allowed me to produce an ergonomic handle I've designed, where your middle finger hooks behind a slight bump for a grip; it gives a more precise hold and is more comfortable to boot.

I try to source the best materials available for knifemaking. Of course steel is of primary importance, be it stainless steel or carbon. Stainless-steel blades are more complex. You have to reach higher temperatures for heat treating them and they also require a cryogenic stage afterwards. The complexity of this process means they usually have to be sent away to professionals for finishing.

Carbon-steel knives are comparatively easy, so it's possible to make them at home. A good carbon blade is also easier to sharpen and can be just as durable as a stainless steel one, the only downside being that it can also tarnish and turn black. Rubbing a bit of olive oil on the blade before putting it away prevents this.

The materials you use for handles need plenty of thought as well. Handles get a lot of abuse in the kitchen (I think everyone knows you should never put a good knife in a dishwasher!) as they are dropped, soaked, dried out, left near ovens or in freezers. These are tests for any handle, but particularly a wooden one. The harder the wood you use, the better. Hard, exotic woods like rosewood, ironwood and ebony, with their high density, are less likely to shift, crack or fade, and their grains give beautiful patterns. There are many non-wood materials available too, from horn to bone to composite materials, as well as a rich list of man-made ones. This variety of options allows the imagination to run wild.

My workshop has grown along with my passion for making knives. Initially I used a corner of the shed – it consisted of a vice, a couple of spanners and an angle-grinder. With the help of a friend I put some doors on to keep Giana's chickens out, and now we have files, a grinder, a drill press, a buffing wheel, a Dremel multitool, a mill, blowtorches and a heat-treating kiln. If I'm missing, this is where you'll find me, dust-mask on, loud music blaring in the background, deep in concentration over the grinder.

Knifemaking at the start of the process is all sparks and big aggressive tools, but as you progress you find yourself becoming more and more of a perfectionist, ending with a precise edge. And that's knifemaking in a nutshell: from a coarse beginning to a fine finish.

HOW TO SHARPEN YOUR KNIVES

A whetstone or sharpening stone is used to hone or grind the edge of a metal blade. Kitchen knives need to be kept razor-sharp to do their job properly, which means they need to be whetted regularly. Whetstones can be readily sourced and they don't have to be expensive. You need one coarse and one fine whetstone for this job and, if your knives are in use daily, it pays to sharpen the blades at least once a week. Here's how to keep them in top condition.

Put your whetstones into a sink of cold water and leave them for 5 minutes, until no more air bubbles come out of the stones. Take them out and put them in a jig, or holder; you can also use them on top of a damp cloth for grip.

The angle you want to use for sharpening is between 10 and 15 degrees. (This angle is calculated by placing two coins under the blade back.) Beginning with the coarse stone, push the knife away from you using a fluid motion, applying gentle pressure on the back of the blade and running the length of the blade edge across the whetstone about ten times. Do this in equal strokes on both sides of the blade for balance.

This grinds away a little metal from the blunt edge and creates a wiry edge, or burr. Pushing your fingers along the edges of the knife, you'll feel this will be more noticeable on one side than the other.

Switch at this point to the finer stone, working your way down the edge using the same principles – equal smooth strokes on both sides at around a 12-degree angle.

To finish off the edge, run it along a leather strop or the edge of a wooden chopping board to remove the last of the wire particles from it. Your knife should now be razor-sharp!

5

THE KITCHEN GARDEN

IT'S NOT an easy acre, this garden. It's perched on a stony slope looking down to the bay. Parts are very wet, parts are very dry, and the prevailing southwesterly wind whips through it mercilessly.

Recently, we have had storms that shredded the polytunnels, and a couple of nasty floods that took the precious topsoil, leaving me with river gravel. I sometimes worry about our cattle breaking in too; the newly planted defences of prickly hedges along one entire boundary are still very young and thin. Having said that, it is an acre of very fertile soil set in a perfect corner of the farm with wonderful views looking out over our land, towards the Fastnet Lighthouse, and west up to a hill with a Martello tower. It is my own plot of land, and a place where I have made my mark.

When I was growing up, the field where the garden has developed was known as 'The Lower Ground', halfway down the avenue from the main house and accessed through a little wood. The garden today, with its earwigs and damsel flies, greenhouses and composting, shares a yard with our busy neighbours in the Smokehouse, butchering pigs and smoking bacon every day, filling vans for the weekly markets and couriers collecting for deliveries to suppliers.

I came to gardening in a roundabout way after I finished boarding school in Newtown, a Quaker school in County Waterford. My brother Fingal and I were members of one of four Irish farmhouse cheese families attending the school, with a reputation on the schoolbus for our tuck boxes full of potent-smelling family offerings. I loathed the loss of my freedom in school and developed a melancholic, lactose-intolerant self-image. 'I'm Clovisse, the cheese orphan!', I'd think to myself. Once my schooling ended I took off round the world with a friend, packing and re-packing a backpack with flip flops or snow boots for adventures in New Zealand, Australia, Cuba, the Caribbean and Canada. On returning to Ireland I set up a small business with a friend in Kinsale, County Cork, where we taught waterskiing and wakeboarding in the summer months. It was not long before I discovered that water was not my element, and that I was only barely staying afloat!

Back on dry land, I studied graphic design in Cork city, developing some knowledge and skills with computer programs and design. Again, this was not a direction I was comfortable with. What was emerging, though, was a sense that I wanted to work growing things, particularly herbs and vegetables. So, by a process of elimination, I realised what I was missing: the land, the farm and Gubbeen.

Back home, Tom (my father) suggested I work some land for myself. We always had a ridge of potatoes, cabbages or leeks in a field but there hadn't been a kitchen garden since my grandmother's time. It had fallen out of use from other distractions, particularly Giana establishing the cheeses and Tom developing the farm. I got planting my first crop of broad beans – 'Aquadulce Claudia' – the very week I came home. They grew and grew, and cropped well. It was my first very satisfying gardening success.

Along with the garden, the timing was right for me to plant a new orchard as the old one, planted by my great grandfather Thomas Ferguson, was coming to an end. In his time, the whole family had worked together to haul tonnes of seaweed from Crewe Bay to fertilise 2 acres around the house, and then small apple whips were sent down from Dublin with a horticultural expert to oversee the planting. It had been a beautiful orchard until a few of the fragile old trees fell, and it bore the brunt of the 1987 hurricane.

In 2007 I came across the Irish Seed Savers Association (ISSA) in County Clare and became interested in planting some of the Irish apple varieties such as 'Irish Molly', a crisp, sweet eater from Cork, 'Dick Davies', 'Kerry Pippin' and 'Rawley's Seedling', among others. Within four years of planting, the trees were starting to crop. They are really a nice feature in the lower garden now, set in mown grass and surrounded by a circle of flowering chives to ward off canker.

The next task was to develop a fruit cage, which I built with a skilled scaffolding friend. Tom had always known the kitchen garden his parents and grandparents had tended, up where the big shed is now. I salvaged old gooseberry and blackcurrant bushes from there and began with my own loganberries, black and white currants, summer and autumn varieties of raspberries, along with jostaberries – a boisterous-flavoured berry, a cross between a gooseberry and a blackcurrant, which is excellent for jams.

My grandfather William Ferguson was a real gardener. As a child, by the time I was just starting to get about the farm and owned my first pair of wellies, I would follow him around his garden. He had cabbages, gooseberries, potatoes, onions and peas. He also loved dahlias, and I remember that he would bring a big bunch into the house and earwigs would scramble out onto the tablecloth. There were young peas to steal, and baby carrots he'd rub the earth off on his trousers for me. His garden was managed the way he had learnt from his father, before the word 'organic' came into our life. Along the back wall he had a big heap of well-rotted manure, and he would put nettles into a barrel and rot them down to make a strong nitrogen feed for the peas. Simply, the garden worked as it had always done, using seaweed and manure composts along with personal knowledge and understanding of the land and the seasons.

In my garden, whatever goes to seed the pigs and chickens will happily take off my hands. The pigs get so much pleasure from the purple sprouting broccoli stalks and the overgrown comfrey, which is said to be good for their digestion and their skin. They are fun-loving animals and it is a real joy to pile big old cabbages into their pens.

Perhaps my first serious influence and certainly my first education about gardening was from my godfather Jonathan Hamel Cooke and his partner Sue Dickinson. Jonathan lived near Gubbeen during my childhood and was a gardener, living off his own produce down at Crewe Bay. Sue is now the head gardener at Eythrope, a country house with a stunning walled garden in Buckinghamshire. I stayed with them and worked there for a summer season. It was a perfectionist's garden, needing lots of discipline and training. Every potting shed built and each vegetable grown had to be perfect. The cherry houses and pineapple houses were immaculately kept. They would even brush a pattern into the dewy lawns every morning. I learnt so much from my time with them, and it re-emphasised my respect for the knowledge and skills required in developing a serious garden.

Shortly after my time with Jonathan and Sue I continued to gain more experience and training when I met a very inspiring gardener, Joy Larkcom, who had come to live near us and was developing her new garden, like mine, in a windy place. She very generously shared so much information with me and I am extremely grateful to her for opening my eyes to so many great varieties of greens.

I continued to gain more experience and training at Riverford Farm in Totnes, Devon, which is part of a very large and commercially run organic box scheme enterprise. Riverford now delivers over 40,000 boxes of organic vegetables a week throughout the UK, all from regional farms. I pretty much developed a permanent icicle on the

end of my nose during the snowy winter months, trimming and crating leeks for days on end. Together, these two working experiences showed me the widest range of gardening, from the highly disciplined traditions of a historic walled garden to a fully commercialised organic business.

Armed with my recently acquired knowledge, I returned to Gubbeen and started on the foundation of what has become Gubbeen Greens. On my first day back, Jerry O'Callaghan came in and ploughed 'The Lower Ground' for me, before we went about laying out every section, picking stones from the field – always the first task in reclaiming any land in West Cork, and one that Fingal and I were well used to. As kids, we would battle about who would get the job driving the digger while the other broke their back loading the stones.

Then there were the perennial weeds, the previous tenants, to be conquered. You really have to get on top of them or they just move in; it is vital to remove them before they seed. Lime and composts help, while constantly keeping the pH balance checked and corrected.

From this point onwards, it is always about maintaining soil fertility, using really well-rotted manures from the farm of course, and requiring trips back down to Crewe Bay with the quad trailer for seaweeds, preferably kelp. Every year I haul it up to the garden after a good storm. Finally, a conditioning crop of clover, phacelia or field beans is planted. These 'green manures' not only prevent nutrients leaching but also fix nitrogen in the soil.

That first year, my Christmas present was a small shed. It became my headquarters, where I still pack my salad bags and vegetables, and where I store my gardening tools, with an old sofa sitting in front of it for finer, sun-drenched summer moments with the Sunday papers.

During those early months, a big investment was my first polytunnel. These straight-sided tunnels from Highbank in County Kilkenny were an essential key to the garden's plan; without them the growing season would be really short and the crops boringly limited. The polytunnels were erected on good, firm foundations and give crucial protection from those salty prevailing southwesterly winds. They have lasted well; it was nearly ten years before any plastic needed replacing.

From the beginning my target was to have four polytunnels, which made sense from a vegetable crop rotation point of view, allowing me to keep disease pathogens down and improve the soil structure and fertility. I built the second polytunnel from the profits of the garden's first year, and the third was paid for by the crops. Two polytunnels are dedicated primarily to growing tomatoes and cucumbers: the cash cows. The third is for soft herbs and fast-maturing salads. The fourth has now had two torrential floods stream through it, so plans are being made to relocate it to a better site before next winter, and for it to be used for an assortment of miscellaneous experiments.

The boundary hedge – the cow defence – is a planting of blackthorn, hawthorn, elderflower, rambling pink roses and *Rosa rugosa*, which we hope will make it as uncomfortable as possible for beasts to break through. Nearer to the main house is a thickly planted hedge of escallonia. Being evergreen, and about 5 feet high by as much deep, it keeps most of the southwesterly winds at bay in front of the smokehouse.

After the last flood I made decisions to undertake some major landscaping. I designed the garden to have two terraces separated by a wide concrete path. Like Gertrude Jekyll said: 'wide enough for two fat ladies to walk down'. This has made these areas much easier to work now, and in addition I have at last levelled off the slope so my precious fertile soil is not running off and feeding the nettles in the chicken run, but rather gives its riches to the vegetables and flowers in the garden.

I like to plant in random fashion rather than in regulated rows. This started for me during my first harvest when I noticed unsightly gaps in the straight lines but wanted to diversify patches so there would always be something growing. There is great value in allowing many plants and flowers to go to seed; they have so much more to offer at this stage, such as flowers for insects, seeds for saving and the plants self-seeding. I haven't planted dill for years as it self-seeds all round if left to finish its life cycle, but I allow a couple of strong plants of healthy varieties to go to seed from every harvest.

In the early days I was so grateful for the power of a mechanical digger in preparing the site here; now I feel I don't want the ground compacted, and so keep mechanisation to a minimum. I am a natural, chemical-free gardener, and I believe that vegetable gardens need a bit of soul. In essence I believe that manual labour over horsepower supports this; big machinery takes the air and friability out of the soil structure, suffocating the bacterial life that is so hard to develop. Saying that, reddening or digging over the earth is back-breaking work, and I am beginning to accept any offers of help with this job; I have a user-friendly rotavator to work my soil, and am thankful for the reverse gear that occasionally gets me out of trouble when the soil beds down too deep!

Similarly, in the dairy, the cheeses, after years of work, have grown their own bio-diverse flora balance. Gubbeen no longer has to import foreign rind cultures. Equally, Fingal is now developing beautiful natural skins on his salamis. We all seem to have the same mindset, working with nature rather than manipulating it.

For the last five years I have followed the bio-dynamic calendar for sowing and planting. As the moon passes through its phases from waxing to waning there are days allotted to the four plant groups: fruit seed, leaf, root and flower. My grandfather always knew when the full moon was coming. He was aware of these things and I have a mind to do it this way too. It brings structure to the timing of the work, and I am struck by how healthy most of my plants are as a result.

I do a lot of companion planting, too, although I am not slavish about it. I lure hoverflies to tagetes, for example, which in return eat all the unwanted aphids. I choose to grow flowers that pollinating insects are especially attracted

to: *Verbena bonariensis* is adored by butterflies and self-seeds wonderfully, both white- and blue-flowered borage, tagetes, nigella and cornflower. Teasel are also great, whose seed heads are often visited by the small birds such as finches and wrens. And of course during the summer months there are the wonderfully scented sweet peas. My favourite variety is the bi-coloured 'Matucana', while Giana's favourite is the pink-blushed 'Anniversary' variety, but all sweet peas are OK by me, their scent filling the garden and drifting up to the house on a breeze.

Flowers are as important as vegetables in the garden; they bring pollinators and colour and scent to the otherwise green environs of West Cork. I am quite keen to grow a dark border too – chocolate cosmos, black dahlias and a near-black ornamental grass, *Ophiopogon planiscapus* 'Nigrescens'. That will be something to look forward to.

As anyone who has ever worked in a garden knows, there are the bleak moments, the 'must do' jobs that can play on your conscience and loom large. Tuning into the seasons and learning the optimum moment for doing certain jobs are vital, as is knowing how to prevent the hungry gaps, to ensure a continuous flow of greens.

Another good trait is learning to cope with the failures: slugs taking over a bed of brassicas or salad leaves, a row of courgettes that either shrink back into nothing or become wind-burnt miseries that are only good for the pigs. All these setbacks have helped me develop a nice thick pelt. If you have to scrap something and start all over again, it's best to learn from it too.

I am lucky in that I enjoy every aspect of it: the pace, the impossibility of rushing things, the unpredictability and the way the garden trickles in and out of the farm and other work we all do.

Grow, Harvest, Cook

One part of my garden output for which I always find a home are the herbs. Thyme, parsley, sage, oregano, basil, rosemary, tarragon… Fingal and the Smokehouse crew are like locusts; it doesn't matter how much I grow, they are down here picking it! The same goes for the flowers. Local restaurants always want little posies for their tables, which is perfect: we give all the lovely seasonal offerings the garden provides – flowering coriander and parsley, cosmos, sweet pea, borage, cardoon flowers which dry and keep so well and decorative gourds in the seasons that the weather permits. They decorate the front of house beautifully.

I have had a very good gardening relationship with our friend Carmel Somers of Good Things Café in Durrus, about a half an hour's drive from Gubbeen. Not long after I had planted up my first polytunnel she moved to Ireland with her three daughters following a serious restaurant career in London. Carmel had met Giana as she was getting to know local growers and producers for her new café menu. She asked Giana if she could get some herbs from me and over the years the weekly order grew from just herbs to all the new crops I was experimenting with.

Cooking now drives my garden. My own culinary experience underwent a serious learning curve when I joined Carmel at Good Things Café, working in a professional kitchen, soaking up the skills and disciplines there. I am always happy working with Gubbeen's ingredients, along with other local products.

I delight in growing things that you can't easily find in this part of the world: globe artichokes, chicories, celeriac, unusual radishes, pea shoots and other influences from restaurants and seed catalogues. Carmel loves these ingredients and designs wonderful menus with them. Most weeks she will ring and say, 'Just bring me everything you have!'

Both Fingal and I have grown up in such a kitchen culture at home that preparing the foods we make and grow is a very attractive side line, and when we see people enjoy and devour our work it is a real joy. A lettuce isn't just a lettuce, it is a salad. Creating an evening's menu from a bucketful of tomatoes still warm from the heat of the polytunnels during summer brings great satisfaction; I can produce a long list of the delicious soups, relishes, pickles or rich passata they can make. When my mind starts to wander a bit, looking down at a row of radishes (I grow the black-skinned Spanish radish and the 'Beauty Heart' variety with its white skin and bright pink flesh), I remember a wonderful salad I once had with my godmother Penny Forster in

Bocca di Lupo in London, where they served mandolined slices of radishes dressed in truffle oil and shavings of hard Pecorino Romano cheese. Lovely!

I use most of my produce now when I team up with Fingal under his market umbrellas, along with the Texas grill he has built, bringing our kitchen and food creations out to a beautiful field or forest, or the seashore. I have 10–20 salads I love to do, depending on what is growing. The farm eggs, the herbs, the beef, the pork, plus local fish straight in from the day boats, are all wonderful ingredients to work with.

I have also been doing quite a few of my 'Gubbeen Garden Lunches', which I devised for Giana as people were asking to come and see her cheesemaking. Once visitors are here, of course, they have to meet the pigs and see the Smokehouse where the salamis and chorizo are produced, before leaning over my garden wall. Often our guests have come for miles, so it was the obvious conclusion just to cook a big Gubbeen lunch, full of Giana's cheeses and Fingal's meats, with masses of the salads and vegetable dishes I love making. I bake bread and ask for some of our cheesemaker Rose's own butter, pick fruit from the garden and collect a few eggs from the hens. I try to keep the dogs out of the kitchen when people are here, but I do suspect that it's part of the fun – we are a farm, these are our foods, and when we are there the dogs are there too. Some days there could also be one of the men working with Tom on the farm who will join us.

I am also on call for working at the Gubbeen stall at the weekly farmers' markets, selling our foods in Mahon Point in Cork City and more locally in Bantry, Skibbereen and Schull. A garden can be a solitary place, so markets are a great balance to get me out and about. Feedback is very good for me – it drives me on and, as with the Gubbeen Garden Lunches, I get to meet the customers and learn if they like what I do. If I have surplus of garden leaves I bag them up for salads, and I bake a weekly selection of tarts including a Gubbeen cheese tart using Fingal's lardons, or an Alsace onion tart. Depending on the time of year, I also bring along jars of my own pesto, chutneys or pickles – all great accompaniments to cheeses and hams.

I get real pleasure from making up generous bunches of herbs, bags full of really fresh salads and boxes of potatoes, tomatoes, flowers and greens for our friends and neighbours. I can see the next few years will be a broadening phase for the Gubbeen Garden and me, its resident gardener, cooking up a future with a stronger structure and clearer sense of sound business practice.

The Growing Seasons

As in any garden, seasonal activities at Gubbeen vary enormously from spring through to winter. On a coastal, wind-blasted headland of West Cork there is little that makes much sense to grow in the winter. Realistically, all that can be done is to plan the seeds for the growing season ahead, allow the land to rest and wait for the gales and rain to stop, and for longer days to bring more light and warmth.

Having said that, the tunnels do tick over with the salad plantings from the autumn, and these keep the family happy. Miner's lettuce (winter purslane) and claytonia are wonderful greens and continue to crop on indoors, under cover, while flat-leaf parsley and mustards keep going throughout the long winter. There are also good efforts from brassicas such as kale, red cabbage and purple sprouting broccoli (PSB), which just ticks over and is ready in early spring.

SPRING

The spring garden is very busy. It is the time of year dedicated to sowing and planting and encouraging growth and variety to make for super-active days of summer harvesting and selling.

The list of produce that can be grown outdoors in West Cork is long but it is governed by the soil type and is very much weather-dependent. Whatever the weather, there will be one crop or another that thrives while others will fail, but without a doubt we always have potatoes.

For us in Gubbeen, the outside spring garden begins with potato day, some time between St Patrick's Day and the first cuckoo call, a tip I learnt from Tom who was told by his father that if you hear the cuckoo calling, the opportunity for potato planting is over. Potatoes will have been chitting in my garden shed from the end of January until planting in March and, depending on the year, I may only plant outside potatoes as I usually need all the space I can get in my polytunnels.

Tom will come and make the drills for me. He works so fast and makes it look so easy; his technique is effortless, learned from a lifetime of experience with the soil and a shovel. I work alongside him, picking stones and hauling out the perennial weeds, before laying down well-rotted manure in the drills from a pile kept up in the farm from the calf shed. I lay seaweed in the gullies of the drills whenever possible, while the urea from the manure is high in nitrogen and, combined with straw, helps make the soil structure nice and friable. Once the spuds are in, I put the rotavator away so I can get on with manual digging and planting.

I do not grow many main crops as blight can attack and I do not spray them with anything for protection from blight as part of my chemical-free approach to gardening. The main crop I do grow and a favourite of ours is 'Pink Fir Apple', a firm and knobbly little spud that many chefs delight in. I like to grow earlies that could be in and out before blight becomes a problem. My favourite earlies are 'Anyas', a cross between 'Desirée' and 'Pink Fir Apple', and I plant 'Charlotte', 'Sharpes Express', 'Aaran Pilot', 'Nicola' and 'British Queen'. There are so many great potato growers around that I don't have to worry about the more traditional varieties and can experiment with more novelty potatoes, such as the deep, blue-fleshed 'Edzell Blue' or the golden-fleshed 'Mayan Gold'. I prefer salad potatoes, which are not a common Irish favourite and so I have learnt to grow my own!

My first love was broad beans, and then peas – and they are always in the garden, sometimes blown sideways by the winds and sodden in the rain, but sugar snap peas or mangetout will always crop for me. They can withstand very cool conditions and can be grown quite early

in spring, unlike the French beans and borlotti, which I have had to move into the polytunnels as they failed outdoors two years running. Another fantastic bean cropper came to Gubbeen as a gift from my cousin Jane Lane in Staffordshire; it is a terrifically hardy heritage runner bean whose name was never given to us but the flavour is fantastic and it has an interesting way of the seeds turning from a bright pink to a glossy black once they are dried.

While many sowings start in propagators in my heat-controlled greenhouse in the spring, root vegetables do not like to be transplanted from one to the other as they will go to seed. Instead, they are planted directly into the ground, which I do on a root crop day within the bio-dynamic calendar. One outdoor root vegetable that is not so easy to grow in West Cork is the carrot; in a chemical-free garden carrot fly is your enemy, so following the advice of many organic growers I sow them indoors early in the season and that means I have them harvested before the carrot fly can lay its eggs.

With leeks, a technique I use is to dig a patch of soil, put down a guide-line to keep me straight, then I bore holes the width of a shovel handle, separating the multi-sown young leeks and trimming their roots slightly, and place one plant in each hole before filling the holes with water. This method is meant to create a better and more succulent white stem on the leek. Another method is to sow the seed direct, close together in drills, and then carefully pull baby leeks out to use while leaving one plant every 6 inches or so to grow on to a larger leek.

During the spring season my love of beetroot returns, starting with little quick-growing varieties in the spring before moving on to more exotic varieties such as 'Golden Burpees' or 'Di Chioggia', with their gorgeous pink-and-white stripes. Radishes thrive in the cool spring weather, their fast-growing nature makes them very satisfying to grow and there are so many fantastic varieties out there to experiment with. 'Beauty Heart' radishes have a glorious pink, crisp flesh which is sweet and juicy while some varieties are small and intensely peppery.

My globe artichokes have survived well as one of the first things planted in my outside garden and continue to crop year after year. The Jerusalem artichokes also do well and although they might die back and leave a gap in the garden in the winter, they come through from tubers that escaped harvesting in the prior season and return in the spring. They make the best soups!

I have rhubarb and sea kale too, which I force with an earthenware protective cloche which ensures the stems grow long and tender as the plants seek the light. My favourite dish so far for sea kale is a crispy tempura.

Tomato seeds are sown over Christmas before they are planted in a polytunnel in spring. I love heirloom varieties for their appearance and distinct flavours, including 'Pink Brandywine', 'Prudens Purple' and 'Flame'. I sow seeds mostly into module trays and pot on into larger pots to ensure they are well established, then, once the polytunnels have heated up (around April) and the plants are hardened off, they can be transplanted to their final position. I collect ash from the Smokehouse smoker, which is an excellent source of potash to scatter on the soil around the plants. Comfrey is harvested, put into a barrel, topped up with water and left to sit and infuse for a month to make a beneficial fertiliser for tomatoes.

I have green thumbs for growing cabbages in all colours, shapes and sizes – they thrive all through the year because of our salty soil. The 'Greyhound' is perfect with bacon and we all love it. I also grow 'All Year Round'. Once the cabbage head is harvested, I cut a cross in the stem as this makes the plant produce a second growth of spring greens.

We use a lot of kale. Red and green curly kale make delicious crisps, while asparagus kale works well in smoothies, or stir-fried with olive oil and salt or chopped raw into salads. Nearly all the kale varieties grow well outdoors, but also thrive in the polytunnels. We all adore and could not survive without 'Cavolo Nero'.

I have Rhubarb chard, beautiful to look at and delicious to eat, that grows right into autumn from its planting as a salad crop in spring.

One of my favourite veg that is sown in spring is the double-act brilliantly named the Turnip Rooted Hamburg Parsley. With its deep root it looks and grows like parsnip but it is a delicious cross between parsley and celeriac. Celeriac itself, which has not been widely used in Ireland until recently, makes the most delicious salt (see page 208) – vital for giving that finishing touch to a good Bloody Mary!

SUMMER

Nearly everything should be sown in spring and growing by summer. The season is busy keeping plants propped up, stacked, watered and fed until picking. However, Irish summers can pass quite quickly and West Cork frequently misses out on any long spells with high temperatures and sunlight. We've had our fair share of waterlogged summers, which isn't really conducive to successful outdoor growing. There is no knowing what the weather will throw at you and planting outside does often feel like a bit of a gamble; if something goes wrong, there is not always enough time left to start again. I rely on polytunnels to get a good head start in the spring and to extend the growing season through the rest of the year. Without the tunnels the garden would have an extremely short season and there would be limitations on what I could grow. Most days during summer the doors on each end of the polytunnels are opened to ventilate them and make the plants stronger as they are 'massaged' by the passing current of air blowing through. The doors are then closed again in the evening after watering.

Regular and controlled watering is very important in the summer. I do all my watering with a hose as opposed to using any dripper or sprinkler system. It is a habit I got into from the start. Each plant needs a different amount of water and some may not need to be watered at all. It is also an opportunity to keep a last-minute check on what may need to be done the next day.

In a polytunnel you can work with delicate plants and grow quick crops. I regularly feed my indoor salads with a small amount of liquid seaweed so that the crops grow strong and there will be quite a few cuts before they start to bolt or go to seed. There are always regular sowings of cut-and-come-again lettuce: gardening books will often suggest every two weeks but I am never that strict on myself. What is most important is keeping a constant succession going, not allowing one batch to run out before the next is ready for picking, because there is a huge demand for mixed leaves and salad bags from everyone in the summer. I love packing big salad bags with lots of variety and colour for chefs at local restaurants, the weekly markets, our Gubbeen Garden Lunches, neighbours and my extended family.

I pick most of my salad with the cut-and-come-again technique, which means you cut leaves from the plant while leaving the roots in the ground (much like a hair cut) and the leaves regenerate from the centre. Certain varieties are better for this than others, but it works well with the broad-leaf lettuces, mustard leaves, rockets, baby spinach, chard and baby beetroot leaves. I like to mix the seeds from the mustards and the rockets together (sometimes some radish seeds too) for an attractive and varied patch. When I pick 'Little Gem' or 'Cos' lettuces I cut the whole head right down at the base rather than pulling the plant out roots and all; after a while there is a second flush of good regrowth from the stump which can be cut again before you pull out the plant altogether.

What will grow outside always has a distinctly different texture from indoor-grown leaves. Outdoor-grown salads are massaged by the winds and cooled at night. They are firmer and stronger tasting. My outdoor summer salad staples are a combination of 'Little Gem', baby spinach, oakleaf lettuce, sorrels, baby chard, 'Salad Bowl', Texsel greens, mustards and cresses, rocket, a variety of oriental leaves and cut-and-come-again.

All down one side of the first tunnel is an area of soil that is always dry in the summer, which is perfect for my woody herbs: rosemary, thyme, savory, sage (both purple and green), oregano, marjoram and angelica (kept at the back as it grows so big). At the front are the softer and less robust herbs: salad burnet, borage,

chamomile, garlic chives and – my favourite – chives that originate from Eythrope garden in Buckinghamshire that grow so straight and have a very hollow leaf and stem; this particular variety flowers much later than other chives.

All herbs benefit from having their flowering tips cut out as this regenerates fresh growth. I use raffia to tie up big bunches of flowering thyme and oregano and then dry them out in baskets or hanging from the kitchen ceiling.

I have learnt that the way you pick basil is very important: if you just pick one leaf here and there, the plant will look very erratic. Also, if it is left to flower, the plant will not produce new side shoots. By pinching out the tips you encourage the side shoots to grow, making a better bushy plant. Likewise, if you see it start to go to flower, pinch out the flowering tips right next to side shoots and the basil will keep growing better for longer.

With most plants, but with peas, sweet peas and beans especially, once they start to crop it is good to pick as much as possible as this encourages new side shoots and growth and overall you get a larger crop in a season. Similarly cucumbers and courgettes grow quickly and can crop heavily if they are fed and watered well and picked regularly.

Tomatoes need regular feeding as soon as the first flowers start to show until they are cropping and the side shoots on indeterminate tomato plants (vine-type tomatoes) need pricking out to encourage good growth. Controlled watering for tomatoes is important: if you are inconsistent, the fruit will start to split and drop off the plant before they have ripened. I bury bottomless 9-inch plastic pots next to each tomato plant and water them daily. This pot controls the amount of water for each plant and also makes sure the water goes down to the water roots and is not just wetting the surface.

Kale is picked by taking the leaves from the side and not removing the growing tip. 'Cavolo Nero' kale can be grown as a perennial plant. When it starts to go to seed, I cut the flowering heads, which generates new growth from the side shoots.

Although I have had great success growing decorative gourds and pumpkins outdoors in the past, recent wet summers have resulted in disappointing failures. They also despise the salty winds that prevail, as do their cousins, the courgettes; we are so close to the sea it is not possible in stormy summers to protect them. They really do take up too much space to grow in the polytunnels, so each spring I gamble and plant them out in the hope that autumn will be filled with the wonderful array of strange shapes and patterns harvested from this Cucurbitaceae family.

AUTUMN

By the time autumn arrives the pace of growth slows and there is time to reflect back on the summer and recall its successes and failures. Autumn is a chance to catch up on the forgotten chores, store potatoes and save seeds from the expired plants for the next season. Winter is not totally inactive, as the polytunnels provide enough protection to allow certain vegetables and greens to grow, but the garden is easily kept in check, weather permitting, by working on it one to two days a week.

Notes from a week in autumn

Sunday

Six men with enormous horse-powered tractors and mowers are here to harvest the silage. The mileage done on the fields each day of harvesting is epic; the toing and froing from the fields to the silage pit make a distinctive rumbling sound that will go on into the night if the weather breaks.

For ages harvest lunch has been at the centre of this annual work. All the effort makes for well-earned peace and quiet at lunchtime, along with vast plates of food and plenty of Barry's Tea and Gubbeen's own milk.

Spuds were at the heart of the lunch today, served with one of Fingal's unsmoked hams, while food for the evening break included several loaves of bread, Fingal's sausages and a huge bowl of my tomatoes. Just as the men were about to go home Tom pulled them all a pint of Murphy's stout.

Monday

Today I was digging out the main crop of 'Golden Wonder' potatoes. It has been a great year for main crop potatoes, with the warmth in the soil allowing them grow to a good size. Thankfully, blight has not been such a problem this year, so there has been little need to use copper sulphate.

I have made a good start on preparing the ground for overwintering with green manures going in. Phacelia, clover and field beans will fix the ground with nitrogen for next summer and prevent the nutrients from leaching out of the soil during the windy, rainy winter months.

I put seaweed feed on the polytunnel salads this afternoon to try to bring them along. It has been the best feed application I have found this year: I like to apply a little a lot.

I joined everyone up at the house for silage tea – they were fed four small roast pork joints from our own pigs and a big bowl of homemade apple sauce. The Aga was hot, which made for delicious crackling!

Tuesday

I dug out the 'Nicola' potatoes today, and I will keep some for seed potatoes next year. Good Things Café and the Saturday Skibbereen Market both take good quantities.

I cleaned out the chicken hut, to make it nice for the hens that are laying so well. I only have six hens down here at the moment, so they are quite spoilt. They are getting plenty of garden off-cuts and bolted crops on top of their usual layers' meal. They loll in the sun and have dust baths.

I made pastry for Tarte Alsace (my onions are particularly sweet this year, thanks to the sun and drier weather), along with tarts for a Gubbeen Garden Lunch tomorrow. They look beautiful; tomato, basil, my true French sorrel originally from Eythrope garden in Buckinghamshire, red onions, Ardsallagh goat's cheese… I also harvested some basil and tomatoes for lunch and made a delicious batch of passata and a mixed-leaf salad – all very fresh and very crisp, just washed and served in a bowl with olive oil, lemon and sea salt.

Friends visiting this evening had pork fillet for dinner served with a fresh fennel-root salad and braised 'Little Gem' lettuce from the polytunnel.

Wednesday
It has rained constantly all day.

I got rid of the chickweed in the polytunnel surrounding the leeks and fed it to the chickens. The leeks had etiolated a bit with the weeds; I should have got to them sooner. Hopefully in time they will straighten up again.

I planted garlic from saved seed into half of one polytunnel.

For lunch I made my take on an Austrian dish called Fritatensoupe, a beef consommé with a crêpe cut into noodle-like strips and served with thin slices of spring onion and carrots added to the broth.

Made up a couple of veg boxes for local delivery which were mainly salad leaves, coriander, potatoes and flowers along with a sample bag of 'Nicola' potatoes for the chef at Grove House in Schull.

My nephews Olan and Oscar came to make chocolate chip cookies and we had a delicious American-style dinner of chicken legs marinated in buttermilk and cayenne pepper served with guacamole and a tomato salsa.

Thursday
This morning I dispatched one of my wedding cheesecakes to Ballyseede Castle for a wedding this weekend. It was very pretty and made up of several tiers: a whole Quickes Cheddar cut in half for the base; a second layer of Coolea; a third of extra-large mature Gubbeen; a fourth of Killeen goat's cheese; and finally topped with a lovely small dote of Milleens. The whole cake was surrounded by eight heart-shaped baby Gubbeens and decorated with apples, walnuts, figs and fig leaves, lots of oatcakes, raffia bows, and my own grapes.

This afternoon I prepared ground in one of the tunnels for autumn salads and took cuttings from lavender, rosemary and scented geranium plants to replenish growth.

Friday
It feels like autumn in the garden today.

I spent some time this morning harvesting wheatgrass for juice, storing grapes in the cold room and picking a hefty batch of vine tomatoes.

We had roast chicken last night with green salad and salsa, so this morning I made chicken stock from the carcass.

I made sixteen tarts for the Skibbereen Market tomorrow: kale, Cashel Blue and shallots; sweet onion; and Fingal's lardon with Gubbeen cheese. With the leftover pastry, I made Tom some pasties for his lunch: lots of buttery suede, potatoes, carrots and plenty of cracked black pepper.

Saturday
Working at Skibbereen Market this morning with Tom and Pete – my tarts sold out.

Yet another very wet day. This afternoon I cleaned all the grapes and fed the rotten ones, along with the pulp, to the chickens. Using my small passata contraption/mouli I managed to squeeze 27 pints of grape juice, which I have pasteurised and stored in gallon containers. It has been put into the freezer at the Smokehouse for jelly and juice over winter.

I picked up a chicken from Dave at the market and made a delicious spicy curry using 'Green Saffron' spices from Mahon Market. Made enough so that Sunday's dinner was sorted too.

Next week should be filled with more of the same – clearing out the old crops and raking leaves to make leaf mould for soil conditioning in the spring. Tucking in and tidying the garden for a well-deserved rest before starting all over again in the new season.

Seaweeds

When Lee Tiernan came to visit us from the London restaurant St John's Bread & Wine as part of the recipe-designing work we were involved in for this book, he wanted to know which seaweeds were available in the area and whether getting some dulse for his braised spring lamb dish for dinner was doable. Yes, it was doable, because Giana rang friends John and Sally Mackenna who are devoted beachcombers and Sally is the author of *Extreme Greens,* a much-needed book on the benefits and joys of seaweed in our sea-rich country. Identifying, picking, drying, recipes, cosmetics – this book has it all. The Mackennas both came over and very kindly showed us what was to be found from our local stony beach, Crewe Bay. It proved to be one of the greatest foraging missions of the year!

I often go to Crewe Bay after a storm to collect the washed-up seaweed for my garden. I had never gone to the beach with dinner in mind, but since Sally's visit I never go down without a pair of scissors and a bag; I've fallen in love with seaweed and find ways of using it wherever possible. As children we always ate carrigeen and other seaweeds would end up in soups and sushi, but these were bought in or given to us by neighbours – now we have our own knowledge, thanks to these good friends!

Growing up here I spent time on many beaches, I thought I knew my seaweeds – but now I have my eye in, looking at them in a whole new way; there are such different flavours from each one. There is not just bladderwrack, there are many wracks, and I know now to look for specific seaweeds in designated areas of the tidal zones, high tide to low tide.

The many health benefits, complex nutrition and great flavours of seaweed are really quite mind-blowing. John told us that no land-grown vegetable has more vitamins and minerals than seaweed: this is really special food. Being food obsessives and writers, Sally and John were on a mission to get us to try pepper dulse, 'the truffle of the sea', and what a glorious taste sensation it was – luckily I have found a spot where the pepper dulse grows in glorious quantities, so I can pick a good harvest for drying and adding to all manner of soups and stews.

Bladderwrack we collect and dry and then make into a powder with a blender or using a pestle and mortar and this I add to breads. Channelled wrack or cow tang I eat raw in a mix of sea lettuce, dillisk and sea spaghetti, Asian-style – lots of chopped ginger, toasted sesame seeds, a handful of my homemade turmeric-pickled cucumbers, a dash of tamari, lemon juice, mirin and a splash of rice wine vinegar. Carrigeen Pudding (see page 126) has always been a family favourite and is now more than ever since we can go to the bay to pick the red algae ourselves.

Fresh Garden Salad

There are so many leaves out there that can be put together to make a gorgeous mixed salad. I like to grow and pick a variety that brings some soft, some peppery, some tangy and some bitter to the mix – and different textures, flavours and colours. My favourites are baby chard, beetroot and spinach leaves for the earthy smooth flavour, American landcress or watercress, rocket, 'Golden Streaks' mustard and Texsel greens for a peppery hit, sorrel for a tangy bite, summer or golden purslane and winter purslane (known as miner's lettuce) for a juicy texture, raddichio or escarole for some bitterness, flat-leaf parsley that brings a feeling of instant healthiness and the broad-leaf variety 'Red Salad Bowl' or 'Red Oakleaf' for nice bright bulk.

DRESSING

Certain things can really make a salad exciting. I love pea shoots or broad bean tips and a mixture of flowers such as borage, coriander, calendula and nasturtium, garlic chive flower heads and sometimes the peppery punch from a young radish seed pod. I would often use the beautiful chive flowers and some fennel flowers to give a subtle anise flavour and delicate onion herbiness, perfect with a fish dish. For a beef salad I would choose American landcress, watercress, wild rocket and a small scattering of tarragon leaves and nasturtium flowers.

Joy Larkcom introduced me to day lilies, which are fabulous in flavour and texture. She also gave me seed from a radish called 'Sangria', which is soft, peppery and has a glorious lime-coloured leaf with a bright red stem.

Mostly my dressing for a fresh garden salad is simply good extra-virgin olive oil, some lemon juice and sea salt, and I generally free-pour and sprinkle these onto the salad in the bowl. I find it so much better to dress the leaves by using my clean hands, which allows a more gentle touch and a better covering of all the delicate leaves.

Flavoured Salts

As one of the all-time important flavours, salt doesn't have to be simply a seasoning. We always seem to have something flavouring our salt pots and certainly one of the favourites is celery or celeriac, one being so quick and easy, the other bringing a subtler flavour. At Gubbeen we use the bottom oven in our Aga to dry out the flavoured salts but a very low oven works just as well. Try making dulce salt or a herb salt – thyme or rosemary perhaps – using exactly the same quantities and method.

Celeriac Salt

400g celeriac, shredded or grated
400g sea salt crystals or Maldon salt flakes

Preheat the oven to 130°C/gas mark 1.

Mix the shredded celeriac and salt in a bowl, then lay out evenly in a baking tray. Bake in the oven until thoroughly dried. Grind with a pestle and mortar.

Easy Celery Salt

1 part organic celery seeds to 2 parts Maldon sea salt

Put a small dry pan over the heat and lightly toast the celery seeds to release the flavours. This does not take long, so keep your eyes on them to make sure they don't burn. Remove from the heat and allow to cool. Tip the toasted celery seeds and the salt into a pestle and mortar and grind to a fine powder.

Dulse or Herb Salt

1 part dried dulce seaweed or dried herbs to 2 parts Maldon sea salt

To make dulce salt or a herb-flavoured salt you must use dried seaweed or herbs – we dry our herbs by hanging them in bunches upside down from the ceiling of the kitchen by the Aga and the seaweed dries in a sieve on the cool part of the Aga and gets turned occasionally.

Simply grind the dulce or herbs together using a pestle and mortar. You can grind them as finely or as coarsely as you like.

Grüne Soße

This simply means green sauce in German. In my opinion it goes well with almost anything savoury, but it is particularly wonderful with new potatoes and a schnitzel. Grüne Soße has egg in the base, but unlike a mayonnaise it is made with a hard-boiled egg yolk as opposed to a raw one.

If you have a herb garden it is fun to pick for this as it calls for herbs that do not get used quite so often. I think it is fine to play with the combination of herbs depending on what you like or what is growing at the time; they have to be soft herbs and they have to be fresh. For example, you could use tarragon instead of chervil or young radish leaves instead of cress. In Germany this sauce is made with seven herbs in equal amounts and you can actually find ready-prepared herb bundles especially for it. Very efficient. Our German friend Cornelia says that parsley, salad burnet and chives are very important and even if you use just those three it will taste good.

Some versions use quark, crème fraîche, buttermilk or natural yogurt or a mix of all four instead of the sour cream.

MAKES 450ML

4 free-range eggs
150g fresh soft herbs – use a mixture, in equal quantities, of borage, sorrel, chervil, cress, chives, salad burnet and parsley
1 tablespoon Dijon mustard or grated fresh horseradish
Juice of ½ lemon, or to taste
1 tablespoon olive oil
200g sour cream
1 tablespoon double cream
Sea salt and freshly ground black pepper

Start by hard-boiling the eggs (see page 222). Allow to cool completely, peel and cut in half. Tease the yolks into a bowl and mash with the back of a spoon until smooth. Discard the whites.

Chop all the herbs finely – I think it's best to do this by hand rather than use a chopper or mixer attachment as the speed of the blade action can make the herbs taste bitter and overblend them, causing the mixture to become too wet.

Mix the mustard (or horseradish), lemon juice and olive oil together in a large bowl. Combine the sour cream with the egg-yolk paste and mix that with the mustard, lemon and oil. Add the fresh chopped herbs next.

Stir in the cream and season with sea salt and cracked black pepper (you can, of course, add more cream to loosen the mixture). Cover and let it rest in the fridge, preferably overnight, to allow the flavours to mingle.

This can be kept in the fridge for up to a week.

Passata

Certain varieties of tomatoes are more suitable for cooking with than others, the 'San Marzano' being one that many chefs rate highly. It's good to ripen tomatoes on the vine: that way you get the maximum amount of sweetness from the fruit, and the sweeter the fruit, the sweeter the passata. I put whole tomatoes through my mouli, specifically designed for passata making. The skins and seeds get pushed out of one spout while the juice and juicy flesh get sent out of a separate spout.

MAKES ABOUT 800ML

1kg ripe tomatoes

If you don't have a mouli, to remove the skins simply cut a cross in the base of each tomato before popping them into boiling water for 20 seconds or so. Do this in batches, dropping each tomato into cold water straight afterwards – the skins should peel away easily.

Pulse the skinned tomatoes in a food processor and then pass the purée through a sieve, using a wooden spoon to press the flesh against the mesh to leave the unwanted seeds and bits behind.

This is now your passata and it can be used just as it is for cooking or as a base for gazpacho or for a Bloody Mary. If you make a lot, you can boil the passata, season it well with salt and pepper and perhaps add some chopped basil before storing it in sterilised bottles.

Sterilise the passata bottles by rinsing them and then putting them in to a hot oven for 10 minutes. I pour the hot passata straight in to the hot bottles, seal them immediately and allow to cool.

Alternatively, you could store your passata in the freezer.

Onion and Herb Passata

MAKES ABOUT 800ML

- 1 tablespoon mild olive oil
- 3 medium onions, diced
- 2 sprigs of thyme
- 1kg tomatoes, roughly chopped
- Salt and freshly ground black pepper

If you can't face the prospect of peeling tomatoes, here's a tried-and-tested alternative.

Put the olive oil in a large casserole pot over a medium heat and cook the onions and thyme until the onions have softened. Season with salt and pepper to taste and add the tomatoes. Cook 10 minutes. Process the sauce through a mouli or a food processor.

terra madre

Onion Soup

There is a reason why onion soup is a classic: it has a perfect flavour and it is extremely nourishing. Our addition to this lovely dish is to break the bread croûtons into nice random pieces, rather than cut slices, and have lots of runny Gubbeen cheese rolling off them, which makes this very good indeed. To get the best results from this dish use a cast-iron pan with a lid such as a Le Creuset casserole.

SERVES 4

50g unsalted butter
6 large onions, thinly sliced
1 teaspoon sea salt
1 tablespoon Mushroom Ketchup (see page 39) or sherry vinegar
1 litre beef or chicken stock
100ml brandy – more if you're in the mood

For the croûtons
Handful of day-old bread, torn into bite-sized pieces
1 teaspoon mild olive oil
80g Gubbeen cheese, sliced

Preheat the oven to 200°C/gas mark 6.

Set your pan over a low heat. Heat the butter until it starts to bubble, add the onions and the salt, cover with the lid and gently steam. Remove the lid when the onions are tender and increase the heat gradually to medium, stirring until the onions turn a pleasing brown colour. Add the Mushroom Ketchup (or sherry vinegar), pour in the stock a little at a time and work any caramelised bits from the base of the pan into the soup.

To make the croûtons, toss the bread in the olive oil to coat very lightly and bake in the oven on a tray lined with parchment paper until golden. Place the cheese on top of the croûtons for a minute or two until just melted.

Stir the brandy into the soup and check the seasoning. Scoop the cheesy croûtons on top of the soup, and serve in the pot from the middle of the table.

Raw Brassica Salad

This recipe really depends on what you have to hand. The different types of cabbage and leaves each lend their own qualities, so don't be afraid to scale down the number of leaves or improvise with others if the types suggested below are unavailable or out of season.

SERVES 4

Knob of butter
400g Gubbeen cheese, finely grated
6 leaves of young kale
6 turnip leaves
Mustard leaves
8 Brussels sprouts, thinly sliced
1 fennel bulb, thinly sliced
1 tablespoon Dijon mustard
Pinch of chilli pepper flakes
100ml good extra-virgin olive oil
Squeeze of lemon
Salt

Preheat the oven to 130°C/gas mark 1.

Cut a piece of greaseproof paper the size of your baking tray and secure it using a smidgen of butter on each corner. Spread the grated cheese evenly over the tray and bake in the oven for about 10 minutes until golden and crisp. Check regularly during this time as the cheese must not burn. Allow to cool.

Free all the leaves from their stems and tear into small pieces, then mix with the sliced sprouts and fennel in a large bowl.

Put the Dijon mustard in a mixing bowl with the chilli and a pinch of salt. Slowly whisk in the olive oil, then the lemon juice.

Add as much or as little of the dressing to the salad as you like. Crumble the cheese crisps over the top and serve.

Minestrone Soup

I love making this colourful soup in late summer when there are so many pickings available in the garden. The ingredients vary depending on what is in season, but I do like to use borlotti beans and Cavolo Nero kale in it. Aim to chop the vegetables to roughly the same small size. Vegetable stock works equally as well as chicken stock for this soup.

SERVES 4

2 tablespoons olive oil
1 red onion, chopped
1 celery stick, chopped
1 carrot, chopped
Fresh oregano, marjoram or thyme (to taste)
1 courgette, chopped
200g Cavolo Nero, leaves and stems chopped separately
1 litre good chicken stock or vegetable stock
2 garlic cloves, finely chopped
1 bay leaf
100g small shaped pasta or orzo pasta
100g borlotti beans, fresh or tinned
Salt and freshly ground black pepper
Fresh basil leaves, to serve
Grated Parmesan, to serve

Roughly chop the vegetables to a small size. Heat the oil in a thick-bottomed soup pot over a medium heat. Add the onion, celery and carrot and cook until soft. Add the oregano, marjoram or thyme, season well with salt and pepper, then add the courgette and the chopped Calovo Nero stems, reserving the leaves. Once the greens have softened slightly, add the stock, garlic and bay leaf. Cover the pot, bring the soup to a simmer and cook for about 30 minutes; try not to let it boil too hard.

Add the pasta and borlotti beans, if using fresh; if you are using tinned beans, they are already cooked so there is no need to add them until right at the end.

After 5–8 minutes add the drained, rinsed borlotti beans, if using tinned, and the cavolo nero leaves. Boil for a further 1–2 minutes until the pasta is *al dente*.

Serve in large bowls topped with the basil and Parmesan.

Purple Sprouting Broccoli, Gubbeen Cream and Pickled Red Cabbage

This recipe makes a lovely supper that will yield more pickled red cabbage than you need for the dish, but it's such a versatile pickle you'll have little trouble getting through it. Gubbeen Cream is essentially Gubbeen cheese melted into cream and reduced – very handy if you have the odd rind knocking around, extravagant if not, but well worth it.

SERVES 4

Couple of handfuls of purple sprouting (or tenderstem) broccoli, leaves and all
Olive oil, for drizzling

For the pickled red cabbage
1 tablespoon salt
1 red cabbage, finely shredded
1 litre malt vinegar
250g sugar
3 bay leaves
20 peppercorns, in a spice bag or tied in muslin

For the Gubbeen Cream
300ml double cream
150g Gubbeen cheese with its rind, thinly sliced

To make the pickled cabbage, mix the salt into the cabbage and leave in a colander to drain over a sink. Rinse well after 1 hour.

Meanwhile, put the rest of the pickle ingredients and 500ml water in a large pot. Gradually bring up to the boil, whisking regularly so the sugar doesn't catch on the bottom, then allow to cool completely. Pour the now-cold liquor over the cabbage and store in the fridge till needed. It may be eaten after an hour or two, but its flavour is best if you can leave it to pickle overnight.

To make the Gubbeen Cream, pour the cream into a pan over a medium heat. When the cream is warm, add the cheese. Allow to simmer and reduce. Don't let the cream boil too vigorously as the cheese has a tendency to get grainy and split. Take your time and treat the cream gently. The result should be smooth, glossy and thick enough to coat the back of a spoon, so that when you run a finger through it you can see the mark. Feel free to lick your finger afterwards of course! Once you're satisfied with the consistency and taste, it's ready. Strain through a sieve into a pot with a lid, or place a circle of greaseproof paper on top to keep it just warm and ready to serve. Any leftover cream will be happy in your fridge for a few days after.

Steam or boil the broccoli for just 2–3 minutes. Be careful not to overcook it – the texture wants to be giving, not limp. Drain well and place on a platter or large plate. Spoon over a generous helping of Gubbeen Cream and perch a tuft of pickled red cabbage on top. Finish with a little drizzle of olive oil. Eat immediately.

Aligot
(Potato, Cheese and Garlic Purée)

Each year we have the privilege of welcoming French university students who come to work a stage, or intern period, to learn the practicalities of cheesemaking, farming or charcuterie. We have made wonderful friends with these students over the years. I remember them all with great warmth as they bring so much to our summers. During their stay, they cook us the wonderful cakes and traditional dishes from their regions, but it is this fondue-like cheese recipe – Aligot, originally from Aubrac, the southern Massif Central region in France – that I make most often. It makes me look forward to summer when the new students will arrive and enrich our table and our work. Traditionally Aligot is made using the Tomme cheeses of the Auvergne region but naturally we make it with Gubbeen.

We always add Fingal's cabanossi, which are rustic, smoked sausages made with rough-cut pork (although he says they can sometimes have beef in them). I boil them to serve with the Aligot and always provide a salad too – and it is wonderful with a good dry local beer.

SERVES **4–5**

- 1kg floury potatoes, cut into even-sized pieces
- 1 large garlic clove, crushed
- 150ml single cream
- 150g unsalted butter
- 500g Gubbeen cheese, thinly sliced, not grated
- Salt and freshly ground black pepper

Put the potatoes into a large pan of salted water, bring to the boil and simmer until done. Drain through a colander, allowing them to steam for 5 minutes to release some of the moisture and give you a lighter, less pappy mash. Gently push the potatoes, one by one, through a ricer or mash lightly.

The potatoes need to be kept hot as the other ingredients are added, so tip the mash in a bowl large enough to accommodate everything and set over a pan of simmering water. At this point stir in the garlic, cream and butter with a wooden spoon, then mix in the cheese.

Once the cheese is fully incorporated you should have wonderful ribbons of cheesy potato. Season as required and serve immediately.

Proper Roast Potatoes

These are the potatoes to accompany roast beef, goose, pork chops – the list is endless.

SERVES A LARGE FAMILY
(there are never enough roast potatoes!)

2kg 'Maris Piper' or 'Desirée' potatoes
5 tablespoons duck/goose fat, dripping or lard
Maldon sea salt

Preheat the oven to 230°C/gas mark 8. Cut the potatoes into equal sizes, as uniform as possible. Put them in a large pot, cover with salted water, bring to the boil and simmer for 5 minutes. Drain into a colander, jiggle the potatoes once or twice and allow to steam and cool.

While the potatoes are cooling in the colander select your roasting tray and set over a high heat. Ensure your tray is large enough to house all your spuds with a little room to spare. If you don't have a big roasting tray, use two smaller ones.

When your tray is very hot, carefully add your chosen fat, distributing it around the tray. Taking care, roll the potatoes in the tray until each one is glistening with fat: this will help the salt adhere to them. Arrange each potato cut-side down in the tray and sprinkle with sea salt.

Transfer to the oven. After 15–20 minutes, remove the tray from the oven. Use tongs to turn the potatoes, then roast for a further 15 minutes. Repeat the process until your potatoes form a rich, golden crust on all sides.

Roast Beetroot and Soused Mackerel/Herring Salad

We are blessed to have neighbours and friends who fish. Finding a bucket of mackerel or herring in our sink is always a treat, the little fish stiff and shiny-eyed, just out of the sea. This is a recipe in three acts.

SERVES 6

ACT 1 SOUSED MACKEREL OR HERRING

4 mackerel or 6 herrings, scaled and filleted
5 peppercorns
2 juniper berries
2 bay leaves
4 shallots, thinly sliced into rings
250ml cider vinegar
175g soft brown sugar
Grated zest of 1 lemon
Salt

Lay the fish skin-side down on a plate. Season lightly with salt.

Put all the other ingredients into a pan and bring the mixture to the boil.

Turn off the heat and allow to cool completely. Immerse the fish fillets in the vinegar solution and leave to souse in the fridge for at least 24 hours before eating. (They will keep for a week.)

ACT 2 ROAST BEETROOT

6 red beetroot
Olive oil
1 tablespoon red wine vinegar
150ml water
½ teaspoon salt
Freshly ground black pepper

Preheat the oven 180°C/gas mark 4. Trim the beetroot tops and check them for any mud and grit. Place the whole beetroots in a small roasting tray, drizzle with olive oil and shake them around in the tray to coat. Add the vinegar and water, then sprinkle the salt and some pepper on the beets. Cover them with greaseproof paper and seal the tray with tinfoil.

Place the tray over a high heat for 1–2 minutes to start cooking, then transfer the tray to the oven and roast until the beets are cooked through. The cooking time will vary depending on the size of the beetroots, but usually it is about 45 minutes to 1 hour.

When the beetroots are cool enough to handle, rub off the skins under running water.

ACT 3 HARD-BOILED EGGS

3 medium free-range eggs, from the fridge

Bring a pan of water to the boil. When it is boiling, set your timer for 6 minutes 50 seconds and gently lower the eggs into the water.

Half-fill a pot with ice-cold water. When the timer sounds, turn off the heat and immediately remove the eggs to the cold water. Shocking them stops them cooking any longer. Let the eggs stand in the pot until cool. Keep them in the shell until they're needed.

TO SERVE

1 tablespoon olive oil
200ml sour cream
8 cornichons, roughly chopped
Small bunch of parsley, stalks discarded and leaved chopped
Salt and freshly ground black pepper

When you are ready to serve, cut the roasted peeled beetroot into segments much like an orange and toss in the olive oil. Put into a serving bowl. Mix the sour cream, cornichons and parsley, season with salt and pepper and blob over the beetroot. Peel and halve the eggs and arrange around the beetroot and along the fish. Scatter a few of the pickled shallot rings from the sousing mixture over the dish.

Start of a Tart

There are two ways to make the shortcut pastry for a tart. The easiest way is in a food processor if you have one, but you can just as well do it by hand. Here are both methods.

MAKES 2 × 30CM TARTS OR 6 × 14CM TARTLETS

- 275g plain flour, plus extra for dusting
- 1 teaspoon salt
- Large pinch of sugar
- 175g butter, chilled, plus extra for greasing
- 100ml cold water

MAKING PASTRY BY HAND

Put the flour, salt and sugar in a large bowl. Coarsely grate in the butter. Rub the flour and butter together with your fingers until the mixture resembles breadcrumbs. Try not to overwork the butter: the odd lump here and there is perfectly fine. Add the water a little at a time until you can pull the mixture together and form a firm dough ball. If you find your dough a little on the dry side, keep adding cold water a teaspoon at a time till the dough firms up. Cover and refrigerate for at least 30 minutes.

MAKING PASTRY IN A FOOD PROCESSOR

Put the flour, salt and sugar and the butter, chopped into pieces, in the bowl of the food processor. Pulse the mixture until it resembles breadcrumbs – it is important that you only pulse the motor so that the spinning motion of the blade does not melt and overwork the butter. Tip the mixture into a large bowl and add the water a little at a time until you can pull the mixture together and form a firm dough ball. If you find your dough a little on the dry side, keep adding cold water a teaspoon at a time till the dough firms up. Cover and refrigerate for at least 30 minutes.

ROLLING OUT AND BAKING BLIND

Preheat the oven to 180°C/gas mark 4.

Grease the tart tins lightly with butter and dust lightly with flour, tapping out any excess. Remove the now-rested pastry from the fridge. Allow the pastry to sit at room temperature for a few minutes to make it easier to work with.

To make the tartlets cut the pastry into six pieces. Flour a work surface, take a sixth of the dough and start rolling it out. To ensure an even roll, turn the pastry often and keep enough flour on the work surface to stop it sticking. Continue rolling and turning until the pastry is quite thin, about 3mm. Roll the pastry loosely around the rolling pin and gently unroll over a tartlet tin, helping the excess pastry into the tin rather than pinching off immediately. With your index finger push the pastry evenly around the rim, pressing lightly were the edge meets the base. Pinch off any excess pastry. Repeat with the other pieces of dough. Put the lined tartlet tins into the fridge for 5–10 minutes before baking.

If you want to make two larger tarts, simply split the dough in half and roll out and line the appropriate tins as explained above.

Remove the pastry-lined tart tins from the fridge and line the pastry with greaseproof paper. Fill the lined pastry with dried beans or ceramic baking beans to keep the shape of the pastry shell secure while blind baking. Bake in the oven for about 15 minutes, then remove the beans along with the greaseproof paper. Bake for a further 5 minutes or until the pastry is an even light golden-brown colour.

While the pastry is cooking, make a start on the fillings.

MAKES ENOUGH TO FILL 2 × 30CM TARTS OR 6 × 14CM TARTLETS

For the custard
500ml cream
3 free-range eggs, plus 3 egg yolks
Salt and freshly ground black pepper

THE FILLINGS
Preheat the oven to 180°C/gas mark 4.

To make the custard, whisk the cream and eggs together. Season accordingly, keeping in mind what other fillings you are going to use for the tarts.

From here you can play with the flavourings.

LEEK AND GRUYÈRE CHEESE
Clean and trim 1 large leek and cut into rings. Cook the leek in a knob of butter until softened, season and allow to cool. Grate 100g Gruyère cheese. Add everything to the custard mixture, pour into the pastry cases and bake in the oven until set – about 20 minutes.

SORREL AND SPRING ONION
Fry 2–3 trimmed and finely chopped spring onions in a knob of butter and then wilt a handful of sorrel leaves on top. Allow to cool, add to the custard mixture and pour into the pastry cases. Bake in the oven until set – about 20 minutes.

BLUE CHEESE, SPRING ONION AND KALE
Strip the stems away from 300g kale and chop them separately from the leaves. First gently cook the stems in a knob of butter or 1 tablespoon olive oil before adding the chopped leaves and cooking until just softened. Season well. Once it has cooled, add the kale to the custard mixture and pour into the pastry cases. Roughly chop 2–3 spring onions and scatter them evenly throughout the mixture, then crumble in 100g blue cheese. Bake in the oven until set – about 20 minutes.

GUBBEEN LARDONS, GUBBEEN CHEESE, SHALLOTS AND PARSLEY

Fry 200–300g lardons (trust me, it doesn't pay to skimp on the bacon here!) in a little oil until just starting to crisp. Remove the lardons but keep the oil in the pan and use it to fry 2 finely chopped shallots. Grate 100g Gubbeen cheese (traditional or smoked), chop some flat-leaf parsley and add to the custard mixture with the bacon and shallots. Transfer the mixture to the pastry cases and bake in the oven until set – about 20 minutes.

SWEET ONION TART

- 1.5kg large mild onions, chopped into half-moon slices
- 115g butter
- 350ml cream
- 6 free-range egg yolks
- Salt and freshly ground black pepper
- Freshly grated nutmeg

This has a slightly different custard.

Cook the onions in the butter until soft and golden – not fried. Let the onions cool. Mix the cream and egg yolks together, then stir the cooled onions into the mixture and pour into the pastry cases. Season with salt and pepper and the freshly grated nutmeg. Bake in the oven until just set – about 20 minutes – and with a nice golden colour on top.

Bramble Jelly

During late summer we are busy picking the blackberries that ripen in our hedgerows. They are a very pippy fruit and so we like to make a smooth jelly rather than a jam with them. They have a nice balance of sweet and tart, and to enhance that we like to add cooking apples to the jelly, which also help it set.

MAKES APPROXIMATELY **1.5** LITRES

EQUIPMENT
Jelly bag or muslin cloth

1kg blackberries
500g cooking apples, peeled, cored and roughly chopped
Granulated sugar

Put the berries and the apples in a large, heavy pan, along with a couple of centimetres of water to get the fruit bubbling. Bring to the boil and simmer, stirring occasionally and crushing the fruit with your spoon against the pan, until the berries are collapsed and have given up all their juice and the apples are soft and pulpy.

Transfer to a jelly bag suspended over a bowl. If you do not have a jelly bag, you can strain the mixture through a colander lined with a couple of layers of muslin. Leave the juice to drain through overnight. I usually squeeze the bag to maximise the amount of juice from the fruit but this makes the jelly a bit cloudy as opposed to crystal-clear, although it does not in any way affect the flavour.

Pour the juice into a measuring jug to check the volume – you need 750g sugar for every litre of juice. Transfer the juice in to a clean pan and add the calculated amount of sugar. Stir over a low heat until the sugar has dissolved.

Boil to the setting point for jelly, which is 105°C on a jam thermometer, or you can test the set by dropping a small teaspoonful onto a cold plate. Let it sit and cool and then push the blob with your finger – if the jelly is ready, it will crinkle when pushed. When you are happy that the jelly will set, remove the pan from the heat and pour it into warm, sterilised jars.

To sterilise jars I simply rinse them in hot water and then put them into a hot oven for 10 minutes. Seal and label your filled jars and store in a cool place.

For best flavour, leave the bramble jelly to mature a bit before eating. You can leave it for a few weeks or up to a year.

Clafoutis

When I was growing up we spent warm summers in France with an uncle and cousins and a great lady called Maurisette who made clafoutis. She of course worked with spoonfuls and cups, as she taught me, and for her it had to be made with black cherries. Being Irish, we use blackberries (blueberries and raspberries would work too). I have always rather admired people who cook confidently without scales – but as a cheesemaker I have a forensic interest in the science of food too. With eggs you need to get the balance right or you can get that faintly sulphurous aftertaste.

SERVES 4

1 large cup blackberries
85g unrefined golden caster sugar
A few drops of lemon juice, to hold the colour
25g butter, plus a little for greasing
Seeds scraped from 1 vanilla pod
2 large free-range eggs
40g plain flour
60ml full-cream milk
60ml double cream
Small pinch of salt

Preheat the oven to 180°C/gas mark 4.

Gently heat the blackberries with 3 tablespoons of the sugar until they begin to soften and some juices begin to leak out, then add a few drops of lemon juice, just to hold the colour. Try not to make this into a sauce but keep it as sweetened berries.

Warm the butter to a liquid, then add the vanilla pod seeds. Whisk the eggs and the remaining sugar in a large bowl, then slowly add the sifted flour, milk and cream, whisking until smooth. Slowly whisk in the butter and vanilla seeds. Add a small pinch of salt.

Grease an ovenproof dish with butter, put the blackberries on the bottom, then pour over the batter. Gently arrange the berries but keep a clean colour to the overall dish. Cook in the oven until you have a lovely raised puffy clafoutis with little blackberry dimples, about 30–35 minutes. Eat it warm, served with cream.

Honey Biscuits

This recipe is from Tom's family cookbook. It was his grandmother's and uses the lovely Gubbeen honey as the sweetener. There were always bees at Gubbeen and in the spring honey would come from the apple trees in the orchard; these have nearly all gone now and the bees are scarce too, sadly, so now local honey is a fuchsia and hawthorn mix.

MAKES 24 BISCUITS

225g flour
170g oatmeal
175g brown sugar
¼ teaspoon bicarbonate of soda
110g butter
1 teaspoon honey

Mix the flour, oatmeal, sugar and bicarbonate of soda in a large bowl. Melt the butter and honey together and combine with the dry ingredients. Chill in the fridge for 30 minutes.

Preheat the oven to 180°C/gas mark 4.

Roll the mixture into small balls and place them, 5cm apart, on a baking sheet lined with greaseproof paper. Bake in the oven for 15 minutes until golden. Transfer to a rack to cool.

Malthouse Sourdough

I thought I had tasted some great sourdoughs in the past and had made a good start at making my own until I was introduced to Tim Allen's sourdough! He was kind enough to divulge every little secret to his sourdough success – a crusty loaf that is full of flavour, light and airy with a lovely chewy crumb. You would not want to be in a great hurry to have a loaf in front of you but I feel it is worth the wait. I think it is hard to go back to regular bread after enjoying the wonders of fermented sourdough.

MAKES 1 LOAF

340g well fed, active/bubbly sourdough starter
200g spring water
250g malt flour – mix of white and rye flour with whole malted seeds (we like to use Dove's Farm 'Malthouse')
75g strong white flour
10g dairy salt

(Tim Allen has his own signature blend of flours but you can make your own blend using the same technique with just as good results.)

As this is quite a wet mixture it is best to use a food mixer with the dough hook attachment. Put all the ingredients into the mixing bowl, switch it to minimum speed and mix for 2 minutes, then allow this mixture to rest for 20 minutes to 1 hour.

Resume mixing at a low speed, around speed 1, as working the dough too fast can result in the glutens breaking down, which is not what you want! Continue mixing until the mixture starts to stick to the sides of the bowl and pulls away in strings. Turn the speed up a level and mix until the dough pulls away cleanly from the sides of the bowl – this usually takes about 10 minutes or so, depending on the mixing speed. Although still quite a wet mixture, it should come away from the bowl in one clean lump. Cover the mixing bowl and dough with clingfilm and allow to rise a cool room temperature or in the fridge for up to 8 hours or overnight. In summer it is best to put it straight in the fridge to rise: the slower the proving is, the better the end result will be.

The next day, clean and dry a smooth work surface and turn the dough out. Do not flour the surface. Let it rest for 20 minutes, streching and folding the dough once or twice to start the shaping and to trap more air inside – do this using wet hands and a dough scraper, but do not overwork or knead.

Put a clean tea towel in a small basket and dust it with flour or coarse semolina. Shape and fold the dough one last time, flour the top of the dough, then pick it up, using the scraper to help, and place it in the basket flour side down. Cover the dough with the sides of the tea towel, put the basket in a plastic bag and allow to rise overnight, or even for 2 nights.

Preheat the oven to 260°C/gas mark 9, or as close to this temperature as possible. Remove the dough from the fridge and allow to rest for 20 minutes. Gently turn out the dough onto a floured baking tray, slash the top with a sharp knife and quickly put the bread in the oven. Mist the oven (not the bread directly) with water. Allow the high heat to give the loaf its initial rise for 10–15 minutes, then reduce the heat to 230°C/gas mark 8 and cook for a furter 10–15 minutes. Finally, reduce the heat to 200°C/gas mark 6 and bake for a further 10–15 minutes until crusty and ready. The overall cooking time will be 40–45 minutes.

To Make Your Own Starter

You will need a container, such as a Kilner jar, that can take 1–2 litres. Digital scales are very useful here as both the liquid and the dry ingredients are measured in weight.

Day 1

Mix 50g tepid spring water and 50g strong white flour together, stir well, seal the jar and store at room temperature for 24 hours.

Day 2

Mix another 50g spring water and 50g strong white flour, stir well, seal the jar and store at room temperature for another 24 hours.

Days 3, 4, 5 and 6

You should start to see little bubbles of activity by now. Continue adding 50g spring water and 50g strong white flour and storing at room temperature every day for 6 days in total. By then you should have an nice, active, bubbly sourdough starter ready to use.

Feeding Your Starter

Your starter is a living thing and will need feeding. Never use all of your starter – always keep a small amount so that you have something to feed for your next loaf. Before making each loaf you want to bulk up or activate your starter, getting it nice and bubbly before adding it to your dry ingredients for baking.

If you are not using it every day, keep it in the fridge, but it will still need to be fed. The starter should keep in the fridge for 4–5 days between feeds. To feed it, simply throw away some of the old starter and replace with 120g flour and 120g spring water, stir well and put back in the fridge.

If you notice a thin layer of watery or vinegary liquid forming on the surface, this is your starter telling you it is hungry. Pour off the liquid and feed it straight away.

Seaweed Sourdough

If you want to make a lovely seaweed sourdough, simply add 3–4 tablespoons of finely chopped seaweed to the mix before kneading. I like to use bladderwrack, but you could use any seaweed you like. You may need to use a little extra water if using dried seaweed and you should reduce the amount of salt added at the beginning.

Acknowledgements

For Tom, Fingal, Clovisse, Rosie and me, that this book exists and is in your hands is really because of our many great friends and supporters, so being able to thank them is a real joy.

Kyle Cathie and Sophie Allen, you have been wonderful, we are so grateful. Andy Sewell, who has come to know West Cork and Gubbeen, thank you so much for the beauty that you have uncovered. Our designers at Two Associates who have miraculously shaped our story; we so admire your work, warmest thanks.

Lee Boy Tiernan, who has not only shared so much time with Clovisse polishing our Gubbeen recipes with his skills until they shone, but who created special dishes for our foods which has brought so much of his St John's Bread & Wine skill to Gubbeen, thank you so much.

Tom and I are thankful for the original strength that we both had from fathers who lived their lives fully and were inspirations to us, Willie Ferguson as a great farmer and perhaps one of the most supportive men I have ever met. Peter Luke, a writer whose love of life was so infectious it touched our lives deeply; the Lane family and those deep Staffordshire roots that have been there for me as a farmer – how lucky we were to know you.

I think it was first of all Richard and Mary Jermyn who told us, seriously it was time to sit down and write our story, and at last we did.

There are the old friends who have believed in us and driven the long country miles to be with us not only in good, but also the bad times, like Gabby Hogan, Myrtle and Ivan Allen, Helen Collins, Billy Jermyn and Monica Murphy – Gubbeen is still here thanks to you all.

Very dear friends who for years would write and counsel and make us laugh at the impossible work it has sometimes been and helped so much, like Penny Forster and her lovely family. Jonathan Self and his caring and thoughtful guidance to us, both through the Slow Food years, and specially with this book, such dear allies, we hope this book in some way repays your support.

Cheesemaking is not a solitary business like farming; it depends on a chain of people all working together, and with a huge amount of skill. This is our strength at Gubbeen – we have always had the most loyal, hard-working and generous-spirited people, from Annabel Konig and Jane Parson who were the very first to help me when I was working on the original cheese, to our wonderful friends now, really an extension of our family, Eileen Griffin, Rose O'Donovan, Monica O'Mahony, Diane Cadagon, Finìn McCarthy, Megan James, Maggie May Marciniak, Françoise Rioux, Siobhan O'Callaghan and Brian Schlatter. To quote Eileen after a particularly dreadful day: 'There's a book in it!' and, thanks to all of them, there was. Thanks also to them for the elbow grease on a daily basis and the fun!

Fingal's Smokehouse is there and thriving because of a team of skilled and positive friends, Robin Benjamin, Sebastian Jardine-Otway, Ronan Quinlan, Greg Marczak and Pete Mihaere. And holding them all together in such a warm and efficient way is Cynthia Corcoran with her smile and always her support.

All the people who in the past helped us build our foods, like Noreen Coughlan, Wally Walden, Cornelia O'Keeffe, Johanna Griffin, Donna O'Callaghan, Gemma Boniface, Anne and Mary Kennedy, Roisìn McCarthy and the many others who over the years have been part of our life, we think of them often with real affection and thanks.

The first customers who decided Irish cheese was going to succeed, and thanks to them it did, these people are still very dear to us: Tilla O'Keeffe, Val Manning, John Field and Christy Dempsey, Michael Horgan, Ciarin O'Connor and Eugene Carr, Hartmut Eppel, Jane Scotter and Randolph Hodgson, Denis and Finola Quinlan, Kevin and Seamus Sheridan and all the many shops, chefs, bars, hotels and the distributors and drivers, all of these people who worked with us and helped us to bring our cheeses all over Ireland, then England and Europe, and later to the US and on. Thank you all so much for your trust in us and your support.

The dear old friends who can't know what it has meant to us to have them at our backs as we started out and as we grew – thank you not only for believing in us but also for acting as advisers, shippers and often guiding us: Chris Jepson, Jeffa Gill, Stephen O'Keeffe, Dan Crowley, Lorenzo Tonti, Denis O'Riordan, Julia and Anthony Neuberger, Anthony and Katya Lester, Clodagh McKenna, Connie O'Mahony and John and Sally McKenna

On the farm it is a solid chain of great people who are there to help us with the land and the animals. Andrew Brennan and Rosie Gingell are still always our great strength and so much more. The many people who have always been there to support and advise: Tim and Kay O'Leary, Michael O'Mahony, Linda Shannon, Derek and James Cadagon, Derry and John Ward – we are so grateful.

The garden has been encouraged and in so many ways guided for Clovisse by knowledgeable and generous supporters, starting with Jonathan Hamel-Cooke and Sue Dickenson, Joy and Dom Larkcom, Linda Shaw-Hamilton, Gavin Underwood, Jake James and Daragh O'Reilley.

One family more than any other have touched our lives for so long with every kind of help and generosity, the Allens of Ballymaloe. Where to start? – of course with Ivan and Myrtle, Ted and Ivan, but... all of them. We are grateful for the many ways they have shared and encouraged us, and always the fun, yet it is one person who stands out not as the famous cook, writer and mountain mover that she is, but for us simply as one of the nicest women we have ever known for her fairness, her energy and her goodness, Darina, and our friend Timmy.

Fingal in particular would like to thank Neil Burkey and Annie Barclay whose professionalism and support helped him untangle the complex and detailed story of the meats and his charcuterie work.

To the educators who supported our knowledge and have underpinned the hopes we had years ago to make Irish speciality food safely and with skill, most of all Dr Tim Cogan who with his scholarship and understanding of what was needed gave Gubbeen its present strength in its rinds – we are so grateful. Also to all the many friends we have at UCC and Teagasc, Dr. Charles and Michelle Daly, Professor Fox, Regina Sextan, Colin Sage and each of the many lecturers, technicians and experts in their fields who support us with guidance like Wayne Anderson, and Jim Buckley.

The great intern students we have from two French universities, L'Ecole d'Ingenieurs de Purpan, Toulouse, and Ecole Supérieure d'Agriculture, Angers – every year they bring enthusiasm and professionalism to our dairy, we so appreciate them. Also our local schools in Schull, Skibbereen and Bantry, which often have young students who come for work experience with us, we are so grateful to them all.

For supporting the background of accuracy on Farmers' Markets, my thanks to Quintan Gargan and Madeline McKeever. For his beautiful language and patience with this old Sasanach, Brendain McCarthy. We are grateful to all the many friends and market stall holders who share the adventures, their small change and the rain and wind of markets with us.

We thank our colleagues, the cheesemakers of Ireland, who from the first shared the many difficulties and also the great adventures of building Cais and Ireland's Farmhouse Cheeses, we have huge respect for you all.

Finally and, for us, most importantly, we thank our community in West Cork and our village of Schull who are part of the farm and a huge part of our lives and this business.

First published in Great Britain in 2014 by
Kyle Books, an imprint of Kyle Cathie Ltd
192–198 Vauxhall Bridge Road
London SW1V 1DX
general.enquiries@kylebooks.com
www.kylebooks.com

10 9 8 7 6 5 4 3 2 1

ISBN 978 0 85783 240 5

Designer: Two Associates
Photographer: Andy Sewell
Food Stylists: Lee Tiernan and Clovisse Ferguson
Project Editor: Sophie Allen
Copy Editor: Stephanie Evans
Proofreader: Ruth Baldwin
Editorial Assistant: Claire Rogers
Production: Nic Jones, Gemma John and Lisa Pinnell

A Cataloguing in Publication record for this title is available from the British Library.

Colour reproduction by ALTA London
Printed and bound in Singapore by Tien Wah Press

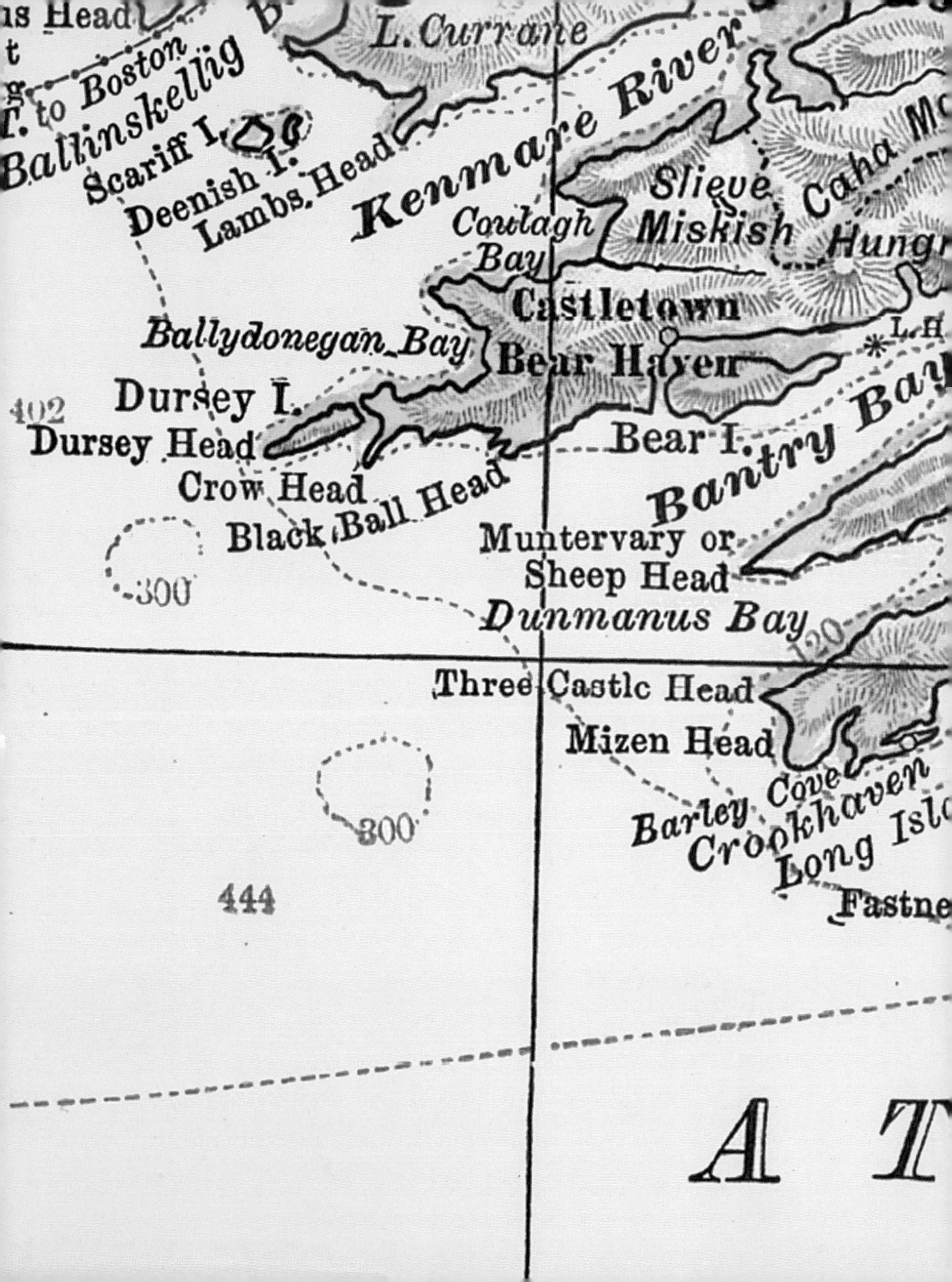

ns Head
T. to Boston
Ballinskellig
Scariff I.
Deenish I.
Lambs Head
L. Currane
Kenmare River
Slieve Miskish
Caha Mo
Hungr
Coulagh Bay
Castletown
Bear Haven
L.H.
Ballydonegan Bay
Dursey I.
402
Dursey Head
Crow Head
Black Ball Head
Bear I.
Bantry Bay
Muntervary or Sheep Head
300
Dunmanus Bay
120
Three Castle Head
Mizen Head
Barley Cove
Crookhaven
Long Isl
Fastne
300
444
A T